# IF SCHOOLS
# DIDN'T EXIST

Nils Christie

# IF SCHOOLS DIDN'T EXIST

## A STUDY IN THE SOCIOLOGY OF SCHOOLS

NILS CHRISTIE

TRANSLATED AND EDITED BY
LUCAS CONE AND JOACHIM WIEWIURA

FOREWORD BY JUDITH SUISSA

THE MIT PRESS   CAMBRIDGE, MASSACHUSETTS   LONDON, ENGLAND

This edition © 2020 Massachusetts Institute of Technology
Originally published as *Hvis Skolen Ikke Fantes* © 1971 Universitetsforlaget

The open access edition of this book was made possible by generous funding from Arcadia—a charitable fund of Lisbet Rausing and Peter Baldwin.

This translation has been published with the financial support of NORLA.

This book was set in ITC Stone and Avenir by Toppan Best-set Premedia Limited. Printed and bound in the United States of America.

Library of Congress Cataloging-in-Publication Data

Names: Christie, Nils, 1928-2015 author. | Cone, Lucas, translator. | Wiewiura, Joachim, translator.
Title: If schools didn't exist : a study in the sociology of schools / Nils Christie ; Translated and edited by Lucas Cone and Joachim Wiewiura ; With a foreword by Judith Suissa.
Other titles: Hvis skolen ikke fantes. English
Description: Cambridge, Massachusetts : The MIT Press, [2020] | "First published in 1971"-- Title page. | Includes bibliographical references and index.
Identifiers: LCCN 2019034678 | ISBN 9780262538893 (paperback)
Subjects: LCSH: Educational sociology--Norway. | Education--Norway.
Classification: LCC LC206.N8 .C45 2020 | DDC 306.4309481--dc23
LC record available at https://lccn.loc.gov/2019034678

10   9   8   7   6   5   4   3   2   1

# CONTENTS

# FOREWORD

Judith Suissa

Reading a sociology of education book published in 1971 nearly fifty years after its publication, it is difficult not to situate it within the analytic frameworks offered by work in the field that has informed critical educational thought in the intervening years. In fact at first glance, Nils Christie's text, now translated into English for the first time, may seem to readers to be of a piece with the classic works of deschooling, critical pedagogy, and libertarian education that emerged in the same period, reflecting, as they did, something of a particular political and intellectual milieu. Notably, Ivan Illich's *Deschooling Society*, published in the same year as Christie's book, Paulo Freire's *Pedagogy of the Oppressed*, first published in English in 1970, Samuel Bowles and Herbert Gintis's *Schooling in Capitalist America* (1976), John Holt's *How Children Fail* (1964), and Paul Goodman's *Growing Up Absurd* (1962), to name but a few significant works of this era, all develop critical accounts of schooling—aspects of which are echoed in Christie's text.

The very title of this short book suggests that the theorist with whom Christie's work may have the most obvious affinity is Illich. Yet Christie was not a deschooler. The distinctions between his work and that of Illich are, I suggest, at the heart of what makes this book both distinctive and still relevant.

Illich's work, while grounded in an empirical analysis of the economic costs and effects of the mass establishment of state schooling in industrial societies, is also shot through with clear normative visions of education and utopian proposals for how dismantling this system can play a part in the transition to a more "convivial" society (see Illich 1973). While Illich's sociological analysis has been rigorously critiqued in the intervening years, his work still serves a valuable purpose in denaturalizing the institutional features of mass state education systems and reminding readers that "education" is not equivalent to "schooling"—a reminder just as important now as it was fifty years ago.

Christie does not talk about "schooling," however, but rather "schools." The focus of his sociological analysis is not the broad landscape of the institutionalization of education in industrial states but instead the much more modest picture of individual schools in specific places. This, I want to suggest, indicates a rather different ambition and message to the reader from Illich's still-classic text, in spite of some common ethical underpinnings.

Christie is clearly sympathetic to the ethical ideal of conviviality—defined as "individual freedom realized in personal interdependence"—underpinning Illich's work. As indicated in his footnotes, he was familiar with Illich's early writing, yet he does not advocate the dismantling of the school system. There is nothing in Christie's text to suggest that he shares Illich's confidence that "we are witnessing the end of the age of schooling," and he was probably not surprised to discover that the rumors of the death of schooling had been greatly exaggerated.

Not only does Christie rarely use the word "schooling," but in fact the word "education" rarely appears in his book in any context other than as a descriptive reference in phrases such as "the education system" or "the Ministry of Education." This suggests that Christie is not interested in defending the idea that there is an intrinsically valuable and conceptually defensible ideal of "education" that is being distorted or corrupted by contemporary institutional forms.

I am not a sociologist of education, and perhaps it is a little unfair to read a work in the sociology of education through a philosophical lens. But philosophers of education are accustomed to both reading sociological theories and developing theories of their own with a focus on conceptual and normative questions: What is the point of education? What are schools for? And what do we need to do to create a better or more just education system? While the absence of any prescriptive statements along these lines may lead some readers to experience frustration with Christie's text, I found this refreshing. What is more, the text leaves the reader with a far more hopeful message than that presented by accounts of the need to demolish and completely rethink the entire school system due to its inherently oppressive, deadening, or manipulative effects on children.

## THE ANALYTIC FRAMEWORK

The book begins with a detailed description of three very different schools, in different historical and social contexts.

Admittedly, I am relying on the translated text, but it seems to me that the choice of language here is significant and sets the tone for the whole book. The question that Christie poses is, Which ends do our schools serve? He does not ask, Which ends should *schooling* or *state schooling* serve? The body of empirical and theoretical work produced by critical educational theorists in the intervening decades has offered ample theoretical resources for answering this question. Schooling, so we are told, serves the interests of the ruling elite, upholds the capitalist ideological apparatus, stifles children's creativity and independence of thought, undermines human freedom, entrenches structural privilege and oppression, and creates docile consumers. Useful and important as these analytic frameworks may be, Christie is not interested in offering the reader such diagnoses or documenting their workings.

One can, of course, ask who Christie means to include in the first-person plural when referring to "our schools." But throughout most of the text, it is clear that this refers implicitly and sometimes explicitly to Norway. We are offered, in chapter 2, a picture of the simple life of a Norwegian fisherman and his family; they move to the city and become cut off from their traditional ways of life. The point of this story is to illustrate the way in which young people, in this historical and social context, have become "useless." While similar stories could be told about rural communities and young people in many different contemporary industrialized societies, the point is to get the reader to ask themselves whether the schools that we have *here, now, in Norway*, are an appropriate response to this uselessness, and how this can help us make sense of young people's behavior. The three concrete examples of schools that Christie discusses in great detail in chapter 1 come from different national, cultural, and historical settings: a French village school in the nineteenth century, a state school on a Native American reservation in the 1960s, and a state comprehensive school in the north of England in the 1960s. What is common to all these examples is the theme of the particular school—a school located in a particular community with its own needs as well as its own cultural and political features, being governed by theories, approaches, and regulations that have come from elsewhere.

It would be easy, given these descriptions, to conclude that Christie is just advocating a return to a more locally governed system of schools, accountable perhaps by some democratic mechanism to the communities that it serves. There is certainly nothing in the book to indicate that Christie would not be sympathetic to this argument, and in this sense the book resonates with contemporary calls for more local democratic governance, and warnings against the commodification and standardization of national school systems. Yet many of the advocates of these changes, against a background of neoliberal education policy reforms and attacks on the public provision of education, are doing so as part of a broader defense of public goods, thicker account of democracy, and vision of robust civic participation. I am not suggesting that Christie would have disagreed with any of these positions. But his project is a different one: it is to remind us that, as he puts it, "the inner life of schools parallels the common ways in which we organize ourselves as a society," and therefore, in any given society, there are questions to be asked about the values and forms of political organization we want to defend, and the corresponding quality and ethos of what the editors, in their introduction, have termed "the public life of schools."

This may seem like a subtle difference, and perhaps Christie's ultimate political vision was not dissimilar to Illich's. But the kinds of questions that his book prompts readers to ask about their own society and schools are foreclosed if one starts out by positing and defending the view that all schools, by definition, have simply been reduced to the function of certification, replacing genuine learning with "the ritualization of progress" (Illich 1971, 40). For on Illich's view, the institutional features of state schooling as a universal model have distorted the essential educational value of genuine learning relationships so that the only option is to dismantle schools. Indeed Illich, as Neil Postman says, is "a totalist, not an experimentalist. ... In the face of what he is saying, what true believer can in good conscience do anything about the schools except try to destroy them?" (Illich et al. 1973, 142, 147).

This view is certainly reflected in Illich's 1969 text "Commencement at the University of Puerto Rico, New York," which Christie refers to, and where Illich describes how "gradually the idea grew that schooling was a necessary means of becoming a useful member of society." Illich goes on to declare that "it is the task of this generation to bury that myth" and confidently predict that "by the end of this century, what we now call school will be a historical relic. ... I feel sure that it will soon be evident that the school is as marginal to education as the witch doctor is to public health."

Christie is not interested in convincing anyone of the mythological status of schooling or its inevitable demise. He seems more intent, in fact, on offering us pictures of how schools can become valuable, organic, and flourishing social institutions than on lamenting their uselessness. In this respect, he seems to have less in common with the radical deschoolers than with the leading philosopher of American pragmatism, John Dewey (1916, 101), who insisted that "we cannot set up, out of our heads, something we regard as an ideal society. We must base our conception upon societies which actually exist." For Dewey (1916, 96), education is a social process, not a preparation for life, and as such, is organically connected to his conception of democracy as "primarily a form of associated living, a conjoint communicated experience."

Like Christie, Dewey situated his philosophical reflections on education firmly within the practical demands and problems thrown up by complex contemporary societies. In *The School and Society*, Dewey (1907, 32) argued that given the shifts in labor and family structure in contemporary society, "the school must become the new 'child's habitat,' where he learns through directed living." Christie's images of successful schools are, similarly, not nostalgic longings for a bygone age but rather reminders of the importance of ensuring that the places where children spend their days are good places to be—places that are, as Dewey (1907, 27) put it, "a genuine form of active community life, instead of a place set apart in which to learn lessons."

On Christie's view, we can and should entertain the possibility that schools could be, and many of them already are, these kinds of places. Rather than seeing all schools through the lens of institutionalized state schooling, Christie urges us to examine individual schools in particular contexts as sites where, if we look closely, we can uncover and understand aspects of ourselves and our society as well as possibilities for living differently. Thus to paraphrase Postman, Christie is an experimentalist, not a totalist.

Illich, in contrast, like so many educational theorists, cannot resist offering his own normative definition of education, which serves as a lens with which to critique everything that he sees as wrong with the current system of schooling. "The dynamic underdevelopment that is now taking place," Illich (1969) argued, "is the exact opposite of what I believe education to be: namely, the awakening awareness of new levels of human potential and the use of one's creative powers to foster human life."

There is no such independent normative definition of education offered in Christie's book. Christie merely urges us to look at what schools are doing—and *what else* they are doing, besides and in spite of the institutional logic identified by Illich, and think about whether they are doing it well or in ways that we want to preserve.

Thus the detail of Christie's analysis is important. In his description of the pedagogical processes that go on in different schools there are, again, echoes of other contemporary critical theorists. Notably, Christie's description of teachers' refusal to build on top of "what the students already know" and reference, in this context, to the idea of students as "empty rooms" is clearly reminiscent of Freire's (1970) idea of "banking education." Similarly, Christie's remarks about children's experience of the often arbitrary and oppressive institutional features of life in school may chime with Holt's astute and at times hilarious observations of children and teachers in his classic *How Children Fail*. Yet Christie does not seem to subscribe to the pedagogical defense of libertarian education developed by Holt, nor to the more moral, children's rights–based defense of the libertarian education of A. S. Neill (see Smith 1983, 64). There are in fact no general claims made in Christie's text about "children" or "childhood." Like the British anarchist Colin Ward in his seminal work *The Child in the City* (1978), Christie is concerned above all to note how the world that children inhabit, and their ability to move through and interact with it, has changed dramatically in urban industrial societies. "Cities are not built for children, cars are not built for children, machines do not need them, and adults do not need them. ... [O]ur society is not structured to accommodate having children around all the time." Christie's discussion of the place of children in contemporary society is clearly informed by his work in sociology and particularly the sociology of deviance. In a society where children "are no longer 'useful' workers," they will, as he puts it, "probably have to be given an extra margin for deviance in other areas of life." Like Paul Goodman in *Growing Up Absurd*, Christie viewed the "deviant" behavior of contemporary teenagers and young people as reflecting something important about social structures and values. Yet while Goodman (1996, 16, 31) became an advocate of deschooling, arguing in *Compulsory Mis-education* that it is simply "a mass superstition, that adolescents must continue going to school," and many young people "might be better off if the system simply did not exists," Christie seemed more optimistic that schools could be the kinds of places that would allow children to experience a sense of meaning and be treated as useful members of society, working and learning alongside adults in their communities. It is this sense that is implied by the book's title, *If Schools Didn't Exist*, which hints not at the need to abolish schooling but instead at the possibility of blurring the boundaries between an ideal model of "the school" and the daily social reality of life in schools.

In short, while Holt, who became a prominent champion of home schooling, believed that "children love to learn but hate to be taught," Christie offers no such sweeping analyses or conclusions. His concern, rather, is with ensuring that schools fulfill their basic social function of providing children with "a place to be." While there will undoubtedly be learning and teaching going on in this place, the main question is whether it is one that is integrated into versus set apart from society, and one where children feel that they have something meaningful and useful to do as members of that society. There are important distinctions as well as overlaps between different positions within the broad tradition of libertarian and democratic education (see Shotton 1993, Smith 1983; Suissa 2019). Christie's approach, if situated within this tradition, suggests a greater affinity with educational theorists such as Dewey and educators such as John Aitkenhead at Kilquhanity who saw the school as a community of adults and children "living together, sharing, loving," and engaged in "useful work" (see Shotton 1993, 109–116), than with libertarians or deschoolers such as Holt or Illich.

None of this is to suggest that in his insistence on focusing on the detail of what specific schools in different contexts are doing, Christie was oblivious to broader theoretical analyses of the social function of schooling. Like Bowles and Gintis (1976) in *Schooling in Capitalist America*, he was only too aware of schools' central role in "granting admission passes to the class structure of society," and was clearly familiar with the body of sociological research where "study after study comes to exactly the same conclusion: there is a crucial correlation between the family's social position (measured as the parents' professional standing) and the child's completed level of schooling." Likewise, he anticipates many later analyses of the inevitable effects on young people condemned to, as Patrick Ainley and Martin Allen (2013, 171) put it, "running up a down-escalator of devalued qualifications" in the shifting labor markets of global capitalism. As Christie observes, "There was a time when primary and lower secondary school attendance functioned reasonably well as an access point to advantages for the minority," and he predicted presciently, in 1971, that "we will soon hear the calls for twelve years of compulsory schooling, so once again everyone will be placed on equal footing." Yet while critical educational theorists have often drawn on a Marxist analysis to argue that schools can and should become sites of resistance (see Giroux 1981, 1983), Christie's reading of these theoretical frameworks is rather more cautious. As evident in his seminal text "Conflicts as Property," regarded as a modern classic in the field of restorative justice, Christie was not a Marxist theorist. While aspects of his criticism of top-down models of state schooling reflect both Marxist reproduction theory and a Marxist theory of alienation, as commentators have noted (Koen 2013, 208), he "does not rely upon the concept of the mode of production as an analytical tool." When he states "if schools didn't exist, society would still need a way to funnel its citizens into the various jobs found in society," Christie is clearly not taking the existing capitalist class structure as given, but nor is he wedded to the category of class as a basic tool for analyzing alternative social structures. It is not entirely apparent from the text whether Christie fully appreciates the satirical intent of Michael Young's (1958) *The Rise of the Meritocracy*. But I doubt he would be surprised to discover that in contemporary Britain, the "myth of Young," as he calls it, is now advocated without a shred of irony by politicians who proudly declare their intention to make Britain into a "great meritocracy" (May 2016). Nor would Christie have been remotely surprised that while this myth is conveniently sustained by "celebrated examples of *extraordinary individuals* who have managed to break through the limitations of their heritage and educate themselves into the upper echelons of society," in the intervening decades, further sociological research has only confirmed the fact that "*most people* stay where they are born" (see Pickett and Vanderbloemen 2015). The 1970s' literature on how and why state schools ensure that "working class kids get working class jobs" (Willis 1978) cannot fully account for the links between educational qualifications and social structure, especially in a context where most traditional "working-class" jobs have disappeared. These links are still apparent, however, and if anything, the ways in which educational opportunities reflect and entrench socioeconomic privilege is more evident in the current era of late capitalism where, as well documented by Thomas Piketty (2014), it is inherited wealth and property as well as earnings that preserve the position of socioeconomic elites.

Yet it does not follow that, as Christie puts it, "If the schools ceased to exist, a veil would be torn away. We would experience firsthand the significance of birthright." This would only be true, of course, *all other things being equal*— in other words, if we failed to make any other major political changes such as the redistribution of wealth. The criticism that state schooling upholds a meritocratic myth while reproducing socioeconomic privilege is contingently valid in societies where there is a significant degree of structural socioeconomic inequality, and a system that links educational certification with access to differential positions in an unequally structured labor market. Political and educational theorists have dealt with this critique in a number of different ways. One response could be, as Illich (1971, 19) argues, to "detach competence from curriculum." But like Christie's tearing down of the veil, in the absence of any structural socioeconomic reform, this may entrench or even increase socioeconomic inequality, given that privileged parents would likely find ways to maintain their position of privilege by giving their children a competitive edge in an unequal and competitive system. Some philosophers of education have contended that precisely because we live in a competitive capitalist system, where education constitutes a "positional good," well-funded high-quality public schooling is essential as a means to mitigate against the worst effects on children's educational opportunities of their parents' socioeconomic background.

As Harry Brighouse and Adam Swift (2006, 488) explain, "The person with more education has better prospects for income and for accessing interesting and responsible jobs, because there is a causal link between education and labor market prospects. But it is not simply having more education that makes the person's income prospects better. It is having more education in an environment in which that causal link holds."

Although Brighouse and Swift (2006, 490) suggest many ways in which the causal link between relative education and absolute income could be eliminated (e.g., by equalizing wage rates), they acknowledge that this "may just not be possible—perhaps only because politically unacceptable—in the circumstances." This presumably explains Brighouse's (2000, 15) preference, in the absence of any such major overthrow of the socioeconomic system, for a state system of education where "the government must attempt, as far as is possible while respecting other central values, to eliminate the effects of social class on achievement." In contrast, James Tooley (2003, 439), a proponent of removing state control of schooling in favor of private alternatives, has asserted that "if there are still limited (positional) goods to compete for," then in a more equal state schooling system, "hierarchically-inclined families are going to be even more concerned that they give children additional educational opportunities outside of schooling" (e.g., private tuition or extracurricular activities) so as to preserve and pass on their privilege.

All these arguments, of course, are framed within the basic assumption of the capitalist state. While Christie does not take a view on whether the state as such should fund and regulate schools, as his obituary notes, he "was never an anarchist advocate of radical de-institutionalization" (Lomell and Halvorsen 2015, 143). In fact, in his comment, "Can we tolerate such a system? Let us, in any case, try to minimize its impacts," he seems to be taking a position closer to that of Brighouse and other defenders of educational justice within a state system, than to that of Illich or advocates of private markets in education, such as Tooley (2003), John Chubb and Terry Moe (1990), or Milton Friedman (1962).

As a growing body of research is showing, in the absence of any radical changes to the background socioeconomic structure, policy reforms ostensibly granting schools and parents greater freedom from central control have done little to reduce educational inequalities (see Allen and Higham 2018; Pickett and Vanderbloemen 2015). In the UK context, recent policy changes in this direction have not been an organic, community-led initiative involving greater local democratic control of schools but instead have gone hand in hand with a top-down system of standards and testing, and a neoliberal agenda that has encouraged corporate and commercial bodies to be involved in the provision of educational services. In this context, as Toby Greany and Rob Higham (2018) observe, despite the government's claims to be "moving control to the frontline" and giving schools more autonomy, the reality is quite different. Increasing levels of standardization, performance management, and accountability measures have led to pressures on schools along with "incentives to act 'selfishly' in a highly regulated marketplace" (12). The result has been "a chaotic centralization" characterized by "winners and losers" (7, 14).

## THE NORMATIVE IDEAL

I have described how Christie's critical target is not "schooling" as such but rather "schools." In a parallel sense, the core of the normative strand in his work is not an ideal of "the school" or indeed "education." For while we are accustomed to reading devastating sociological critiques of schooling or state education, there are also many arguments by philosophers or theorists of education that defend an ideal of the school or education. Again, this is not Christie's approach.

Christie is not searching for or articulating some essence of the school qua school—a project that has received considerable philosophical attention in recent years, notably in the work of Jan Masschelein and Maarten Simons. In their book, *In Defence of the School: A Public Issue*, Masschelein and Simons (2012, 36) are concerned to defend "the school" as a distinct social institution, which they see as characterized by its essential mode of "suspension"—a notion that "not only implies the temporary interruption of (past and future) time, but also the removal of expectations, requirements, roles and duties connected to a given space." This approach, it seems to me, is significantly different from that of Christie, who far from delighting in what makes "the school" distinct as an institutional form, is concerned to make the point that whatever it is that schools are doing, they will not be good places for children to be if they fail to respond to the conditions of social life within the communities where they are situated. Some recent work in the field of social justice education could be seen as taking a similar approach (see, e.g., Paris and Alim 2017). On Christie's view, schools can be organic elements of society, and not, in Masschelein and Simons's (2012, 36) phrase, a "pure medium or middle" set apart from it.

In this respect, Christie's account resonates with Dewey's (1907, 21) view that most of the problems plaguing schools are a result of "an inability to appreciate the social environment that we live in." In fact, the following passage, from Christie's text, could almost have been taken from Dewey: "We must therefore, to a much greater extent, begin to view our schools as social communities. Schools can and must do more than prepare and qualify students for the life that lies ahead of them. Schools *are in their own right* an essential part of life." In contrast to Masschelein and Simons's emphasis on "the scholastic" and "study," Christie insists that "the public school must first and foremost be a place to be, before it is a place to learn."

In arguing that "the challenge facing the school must therefore be to offer the option of participation—and hereby opportunities to find meaning—within a social system in which ordinary life is represented to the greatest possible extent," Christie is clearly articulating a view close to that of Ward. In his collection of seminars titled *Talking Schools*, Ward (1995, 107, 106) describes schools "not [as] a special place, but simply a particular user of every public space," where "the daily lives of the community and its children are inextricably mixed, just as they were for most people all through history." Ward contrasted this view with the way in which schools have become, in the modern world, "separate and segregated ghettos" (106).

Like Masschelein and Simons, other contemporary philosophers of education have articulated and defended accounts of "education as a practice in its own right," arguing, like Pádraig Hogan (2011), that the inherent values and virtues of education are obscured by the suggestion that educational values must be derived from "particular individuals and groups." For Christie, in contrast, as for most radical education theorists, it makes no sense to articulate the aims or values of any educational practice independently of those of the social setting in which it is taking place.

Work in the philosophy of education over the past fifty years in fact abounds with discussions of "the aims of education" (see White 1982; Marples 1999). This approach reflects a way of thinking about education that is entirely alien to that of Christie, who is not interested in articulating, much less defending, a normative view of what education, or good education, should look like.

This perspective is most evident in the fifth chapter, "A Different School." Rather than focusing on a single line of argument—for example, social inequality, critical thinking, genuine learning, or children's freedom—Christie offers here an important warning against the lure of educational ideals—"the small school" or "free school"—and totalizing systems. For as he says, "'Open schools' may be open for both good and evil."

None of this is to suggest that Christie is shying away from the idea that we need to consider the purpose of schools in contemporary society. Like John White (1982, 1990), whose work has focused on the attempt to articulate and defend the aims of a national curriculum in a liberal state, Christie warns against the danger of assuming that questions about any such "aims" have been settled. White has analyzed how academic subjects became part of the curriculum of state schools for historical and political reasons (see White 2006; Reiss and White 2013). Christie's remarks on how "school subjects are chosen because they have been chosen before, and because we have teachers educated in these subjects to serve as instructors," are almost identical to Reiss and White's (2013, 1) argument that "a subject-led curriculum, especially at secondary level, starts with, and so is necessarily constrained by, the availability of teachers capable of teaching certain subjects." Yet while Christie insists that any discussion about what schools should be doing should be informed by an "analysis of the actual needs of our children today," unlike White, he seems skeptical of the idea that such an analysis will and should lead to the formulation of a coherent set of specific aims for all schools, "derived" from an aims-led curriculum based on an account of human flourishing. Christie was clearly far more open to the idea that different communities and schools should be able to determine their own curricula—a position that has been explicitly rejected by White (2004, 20), who defends the idea of "putting aims and curricula—at a macro level—under political rather than professional control" as part of the aim of fostering a democratic society.

If there is any substantive moral and political orientation informing Christie's work, it does seem to be a version of communitarianism. His discussion emphasizes, time and time again, the importance of collaborative social engagement as crucial to both individual and social flourishing. Human beings, he reminds us, in defending the need for parents and children to be involved in the governance and content of their schools, "do not gather voluntarily unless they have something to give or there is some benefit to be derived from their being together." He quotes approvingly George Homans's (1951, 72) work, which "illustrates how communal life dissipates as decision-making capacities are removed from the municipality," again echoing Dewey's (1907, 28) view that "a society is a number of people held together because they are working along common lines, in a common spirit, and with reference to common aim."

Yet while Christie's analysis echoes Dewey's (1916, 96) defense of the school as a democratic community, or "form of associated living, a conjoint communicated experience," he goes further than Dewey in arguing that "if the school is to nurture cooperation, it must be granted dominion over its own life. ... The main issue is to establish a situation—a system—where all important decisions are made within, or in close proximity to, each individual school." This analysis can be read as aligned with contemporary critiques of neoliberal state education, and Christie would probably have been enthusiastic about recent initiatives toward greater local control and democratic governance of schools, such as the Porto Alegre experiment (see Gandin and Apple 2002). There is no doubt that some of the features of top-down state schooling systems that Christie was critical of have intensified in the era of advanced global capitalism and neoliberal education policy, where, as critics such as Stephen Ball (2016, 1046) have analyzed, "management is altering social connections and power relations to less democratic and caring forms." In light of these reforms, critics like Ball (2016, 1046) have called on teachers to "become increasingly critically reflexive, politically aware and ... reawaken to their real educational work—the ethical and moral project that most signed up to but which has since become lost."

While the breaking up of the state system has led, as researchers have demonstrated, not to more local democratic control but instead often to projects of more top-down control by distant corporate entities, many such critics have defended state-funded education as a public good against an agenda of increasing privatization and marketization (see Ball 2013; Fielding and Moss 2011).

Christie, while sharing the more expansive notion of "public" education articulated by some writers in this field (see, e.g., Lawson and Spours 2011), was clearly suspicious of any centralizing educational agenda on the part of the state:

"If our mission is to create a thriving school community of cooperating individuals," he argued, "the first requirement must be to do away with the system's structure of a giant stepladder with a control center dictating activities from above."

As mentioned earlier, Christie evidently shares some of Illich's ideas about conviviality. The authors (Lomell and Halvorsen 2015, 143) of an obituary and review of his work note that Christie's communitarian position was first expressed "in a rather rudimentary form in 'Conflict as Property,'" and reflected later in his criminology work, where he discussed criminalization and levels of crime in the context of societies that had developed "from closely knit entities, characterized by primary control embedded in interactions between identifiable persons, to the urban cities of late modernity, characterized by secondary control of countless interactions between strangers."

Interestingly, David Hargreaves (1994, 9), author of the famous 1967 "Lumley" study that Christie quotes (see Hargreaves 1967), expressed something close to Christie's experimentalism in a much later piece of writing:

> Utopian social engineering—defining an ideal, such as comprehensive schooling or market mechanisms, and then sticking fast to a national blueprint to achieve an ideal—will no longer do. We have had 30 years of it in education and it has not worked well. We need a large dose of what Karl Popper calls the piecemeal approach to reform—detecting weaknesses and failures and then undertaking the necessary experiments and re-adjustments to set things right.

Although Popper's characterization of utopianism is highly problematic (see Webb 2013), Christie's approach

does in fact reflect a similar resistance to the idea of utopian engineering. Far from being antiutopian, though, this
approach is utopian in the sense reflected in the work of
Ward and Goodman, whose anarchist and utopian orientation was expressed in the importance they attached to "exercising agency in immediate temporal and spatial contexts,"
and formulating "a political approach that values proximity not only in relation to the temporal context but also the
material environments of life" (Honeywell 2007, 240). Christie's book exemplifies both the utopian hope and belief in
substantive visions of a better society, and the anarchist view
that "there is no final struggle, only a number of partisan
struggles on a variety of fronts" (Ward 1995, 26). For if, as
Christie argues, schools are not just mirrors of society, "it
seems only reasonable to attempt to promote change on several fronts at the same time."

Likewise, Christie clearly shares the social anarchist faith
that "given a common need, a collection of people will, by
trial and error, by improvisation and experiment, evolve
order out of the situation—this order being more durable
and more closely related to their needs than any kind of
externally imposed authority could provide" (Ward 1973,
31). This view, alongside the Deweyan insistence on schools
as aspects of community life, is captured in Christie's words:
"a wealth of experience demonstrates that most people manage to find a way to function if they need to, if they are left
to their own devices. In such instances, the search in its own
right for this way of functioning would become one of the
main purposes of school—that is, learning to function as a
community through life experience."

## PRACTICAL PROPOSALS

Christie's insistence on the need for schools to become more fully integrated in, rather than set apart from, contemporary society includes valuable concrete proposals for how this could work. He argues persuasively that "the more schools become places for authentic engagement with important elements of the surrounding world, the more this surrounding world would be invited to engage," and observes that in their endeavor to find tasks through which to enact this engagement, schools "probably won't have to look very far." Lamenting the "grotesque [situation] that nursing homes and schools [can be] located across the street from each other," without engaging with each other, he suggests that schools could get pupils to help with the care work, thereby creating "meaningful tasks" for them.

Interestingly, such proposals have been made and tried in various places, as a recent article in the *Guardian* describes. Yet such initiatives, it seems, are driven less by a belief in "a mode of existence in which the societal nature of schools has permeated our local communities that, having opened up to life, will no longer need special schemes to store their children somewhere separate from the society of which they are part" than by an attempt to address the major social problem of how to care for the elderly—a group of people who, like children, have apparently become a category to be dealt with and "stowed away" (Sheppard 2017).

To the extent that Christie, in 1971, was envisaging a future for society and education, he seemed fairly optimistic. Predicting that "the number of manual tasks to be done is on the decline," he noted that this would "increase surplus and uselessness—but it will help shift the attention to other people and away from things"; in this context, if schools can "educate students in how to *be together with other people*," this would instill "hope."

This is different from the utopian vision of the future offered by recent critics and postcapitalist theorists, who predict how the inevitable growth of population surplus to the requirements of global capitalism and rapid development of technology will render human workers redundant.

On the basis of such an analysis, Nick Srnicek and Alex Williams have proposed a manifesto, demanding full automation, reduction of the working week, provision of a basic income, and diminishment of the work ethic, replacing the aspiration to full employment with a call for full unemployment. Although it is notable that unlike Christie, Srnicek and Williams (2016, 141) do not even mention children, they refer to education, within this analysis, as "a key institution for transforming neoliberal hegemony."

Christie's remarks may suggest a similar analysis of a postcapitalist future, but his corresponding view of the role of schools in society is far removed from this utopian vision. To the extent that Christie is a utopian thinker, he is so in a sense far closer to Myrna Breitbart's (2014, 182) description of Ward as a "non-utopian utopian." In fact, Christie's optimism, perhaps strangely, bears similarities with the view expressed by David Blacker, a contemporary theorist who offers a bleak analysis of the inevitable futility of the institution of state schooling under advanced capitalism, where the growth of surplus populations will consign millions to the ranks of the precariat. In the face of this analysis, he does not advocate an alternative utopian hegemony. What is more,

Blacker (2013, 224) dismisses left-wing visions of education activism aimed at social justice as "both futile and a misallocation of attention and energy."

Christie's work transcends the choice, presented by Srnicek and Williams, between large-scale reform versus "horizontalism" as well as avoiding an escapist route into Blacker's "islands of hope." His text, in fact, is performing an important educational function similar to the work of anarchist thinkers like Goodman and Ward, who, as Breitbart (2014, 181) notes, attached great value to "drawing our attention to the possibilities for social and environmental change *already present* in people and their everyday environments."

In the epilogue, Christie describes a particular educational community that, in his view, illustrates a way of learning and living together that in being "beneficial for 'special' people, ... will also be so good for everyone else." As Ward (1995, 106) noted, "It requires an immense effort to insert a school in to the fabric of a community." As an educator as well as a theorist, one of the valuable things that Christie did was to take his pupils to see and experience such a school for themselves. Having concluded that if this book has value today, it is in calling us to look more critically, but also less cynically and more carefully, at some of the ordinary and also extraordinary schools around us, I decided to heed Christie's call. Remarkably, when I looked up the Camphill movement, to which the school that he described in 1971 belongs, it turned out that there are several such centers in England. One is about a forty-minute drive from my home. I emailed to ask if I could go and visit, and received a polite reply from the administrator. The center had an open day in June, she informed me, and I was welcome to come then. In Norway in the 1970s, Christie could apparently just "take his students" to such schools to spend time with the pupils and teachers in the community, and get a sense of their everyday life, rather than being given a tour on an open day. So perhaps for people in 1970s' Norway, the idea of schools as organic elements of their community sounded less radical. Yet even in England in 2020, there are many schools, teachers, and children trying together to create "a place to be, before it is a place to learn."

Christie's text can play an important role in offering us a reminder of the need to look properly at such places and consider their value. In an age when we are surrounded by totalizing visions of how we can fix social and individual problems through education, and cynical narratives about how pointless it is to try, recognizing such value may be possible only if we acknowledge, with Christie, that "we must recognize that we, along with our schools, are works in progress."

## REFERENCES

Ainley, P., and M. Allen. 2013. "Running Up a Down Escalator in the Middle of a Class Structure Gone Pear-Shaped." *Sociological Research Online* 18 (1): 1–8.

Allen, R., and R. Higham. 2018. "Quasi-Markets, School Diversity and Social Selection: Analysing the Case of Free Schools in England, Five Years On." *London Review of Education* 16 (2): 191–213.

Ball, S. 2013. "Education, Justice and Democracy: The Struggle over Ignorance and Opportunity." London: Centre for Labour and Social Studies.

Ball, S. 2016. "Neoliberal Education? Confronting the Slouching Beast." *Policy Futures in Education* 14 (8): 1046–1059.

Blacker, D. 2013. *The Falling Rate of Learning and the Neoliberal Endgame.* Winchester, UK: Zero Books.

Bowles, S., and H. Gintis. 1976. *Schooling in Capitalist America: Educational Reform and the Contradictions of Economic Life.* New York: Basic Books.

Breitbart, M. M. 2014. "Inciting Desire, Ignoring Boundaries and Making Space: Colin Ward's Considerable Contribution to Radical Pedagogy, Planning and Social Change." In *Education, Childhood and Anarchism: Talking Colin Ward,* edited by C. Burke and K. Jones, 175–185. London: Routledge.

Brighouse, H. 2000. *School Choice and Social Justice.* New York: Oxford University Press.

Brighouse, H., and A. Swift. 2006. "Equality, Priority, and Positional Goods," *Ethics* 16 (3): 471–497.

Chubb, J. E., and T. M. Moe. 1990. *Politics, Markets, and America's Schools.* Washington, DC: Brookings Institution.Dewey, J. 1916. *Democracy and Education.* New York: Macmillan Company.

Dewey, J. 1907. *The School and Society.* Chicago: University of Chicago Press.

Fielding, M., and P. Moss. 2011. *Radical Education and the Common School: A Democratic Alternative.* Abingdon, UK: Routledge.

Freire, P. 1970. *Pedagogy of the Oppressed.* London: Continuum.

Friedman, M. 1962. *Capitalism and Freedom.* Chicago: University of Chicago Press.

Gandin, L. A., and M. Apple. 2002. "Thin versus Thick Democracy in Education: Porto Alegre and the Creation of Alternatives to Neo-Liberalism." *International Studies in Sociology of Education* 12 (2): 99–116.

Giroux, H. 1981. *Ideology, Culture and the Process of Schooling.* London: Falmer Press.Giroux, H. 1983. *Theory and Resistance in Education.* South Hadley, MA: Bergin and Garvey.

Goodman, P. 1962. *Growing Up Absurd: Problems of Youth in the Organized System.* New York: Vintage Books.

Goodman, P. 1966. *Compulsory Mis-education and the Community of Scholars*. New York: Vintage Books.

Greany, T., and R. Higham. 2018. *Hierarchy, Markets and Networks: Analysing the "Self-Improving School-Led System" Agenda in England and the Implications for Schools*. London: UCL IOE Press.

Hargreaves, D. 1967. *Social Relations in a Secondary School*. London: Routledge and Kegan Paul.

Hargreaves, D. 1994. *The Mosaic of Learning: Schools and Teachers for the Next Century*. New London: Demos.

Hogan, P. 2011. "The Ethical Orientations of Education as a Practice in Its Own Right." *Ethics and Education* 6 (1): 27–40.

Holt, J. 1964. *How Children Fail*. London: Penguin.

Homans, G. C. 1951. *The Human Group*. London: Routledge.

Honeywell, C. 2007. "Utopianism and Anarchism." *Journal of Political Ideologies* 12 (3): 239–254.

Illich I. 1969. "Outwitting the 'Developed' Countries." *New York Review of Books*, November 6.

Illich, I. 1971. *Deschooling Society*. Middlesex, UK: Penguin.

Illich, I. 1973. *Tools for Conviviality*. London: Calder and Boyars.

Illich, I., et al. 1973. *After Deschooling, What?* London: Harper and Row.

Koen, R. 2013. "All Roads Lead to Property: Pashukanis, Christie and the Theory of Restorative Justice." *Potchefstroom Electronic Law Journal* 16 (3): 187–235.

Lawson, N., and K. Spours. 2011. "Education for the Good Society: An Expansive Vision." *Education for the Good Society: The Values and Principles of a New Comprehensive Vision*, edited by N. Lawson and K. Spours, 8–13. London: Compass.

Lomell, H. M., and V. Halvorsen. 2015. "Nils Christie, 1928–2015." *Journal of Scandinavian Studies in Criminology and Crime Prevention* 16 (2): 142–144.

Marples, R., ed. 1999. *The Aims of Education*. London: Routledge.

Masschelein, J., and M. Simons. 2013. *In Defence of the School: A Public Issue*. Leuven: Education, Culture and Society Publishers.

May, T. 2016. "Britain: The Great Meritocracy." Speech, UK Department of Education, September 9.

Paris, D., and H. S. Alim, eds. *Culturally Sustaining Pedagogies: Teaching and Learning for Justice in a Changing World*. New York: Teachers College Press.

Pickett, K., and L. Vanderbloemen. 2015. "Mind the Gap: Tackling Social and Educational Inequality." Cambridge, UK: Cambridge Primary Review Trust.

Piketty, T. 2014. *Capital in the Twenty-First Century*. Cambridge, MA: Harvard University Press.

Reiss, M. J., and J. White. 2013. *An Aims-Based Curriculum: The Significance of Human Flourishing for Schools*. London: Institute of Education Press.

Sheppard. E. 2017. "'It's Like Being Reborn': Inside the Care Home Opening Its Doors to Toddlers," *Guardian*, September 6.

Shotton, J. 1993. *No Master High or Low; Libertarian Education and Schooling in Britain, 1890–1990*. Bristol, UK: LibEd.

Smith, M. 1983. *The Libertarians and Education*. London: George Allen and Unwin.

Srnicek, N., and A. Williams. 2016. *Inventing the Future: Postcapitalism and a World without Work*. London: Verso.

Suissa, J. 2019. "Anarchist Education." In *The Palgrave Handbook of Anarchism*, edited by C. Levy and M. S. Adams, 511–530. Cham, Switzerland: Palgrave Macmillan.

Tooley, J. 2003. "Why Harry Brighouse Is Nearly Right about the Privatization of Education." *Journal of Philosophy of Education* 37 (3): 427–447.

Ward, C. 1973. *Anarchy in Action*. London: Freedom Press.

Ward, C. 1978. *The Child in the City*. London: Bedford Square Press.

Ward, C. 1995. *Talking Schools*. London: Freedom Press.

Webb, D. 2013. "Critical Pedagogy, *Utopia* and Political (Dis)engagement." *Power and Education* 5 (3): 280–290.

White, J. 1982. *The Aims of Education Restated*. London: Routledge and Kegan Paul.

White, J. 1990. *Education and the Good Life: Beyond the National Curriculum*. London: Logan Page.

White, J. 2004. "Shaping a Curriculum." In *Rethinking the School Curriculum: Values, Aims and Purpose*, edited by J. White, 20–29. Abingdon, UK: Routledge.

White, J. 2006. *Intelligence, Destiny and Education: The Ideological Origins of Intelligence Testing*. London: Routledge.

Willis, D. 1978. *Learning to Labour: How Working Class Kids Get Working Class Jobs*. Abingdon, UK: Routledge.

Young, M. 1958. *The Rise of the Meritocracy, 1870–2033*. London: Thames and Hudson.

# THE PUBLIC LIFE OF SCHOOLS: EDITORS' INTRODUCTION

## Lucas Cone and Joachim Wiewiura

Nils Christie was born in Oslo on February 24, 1928, to local shop owners Ragnvald Christie and Ruth Hellum. Brought up in a context of widespread political turmoil before and during World War II, Christie took up an early interest in understanding the nature, development, and governance of violence and justice. After receiving his diploma from Berg gymnasium in 1946 and completing a brief spell as a journalist, he enrolled at the Institute of Sociology at the University of Oslo. As Christie notes in an interview reflecting back on his early work, the immediate worries permeating much sociological literature on violence and justice at the time played a key role in shaping the questions that would stay with him throughout his celebrated career: What does it take for a person to treat another human being like an animal? What are the roots of harboring concern and empathy for others, and how do or can societal institutions contribute to reinforcing these positive forces? In 1959, Christie's doctoral dissertation became the first of many works presenting Christie's profoundly original approach to examining—and reframing—these questions.[1] Preempting his later appointment as Norway's first professor of criminology in 1966 at the University of Oslo, Christie's (1960) documentation of the lives and experiences of young law offenders was central in shifting the Norwegian debates on incarceration toward a more humanistic focus on the people involved. In the following decades up until his untimely death in a streetcar accident in 2015, he helped a generation of sociologists, criminologists, and educators "see further and wider, beyond the short-sighted and pre-categorized."[2] *If Schools Didn't Exist* (first published in 1971), whose arguments for autonomous schools were widely influential in shaping the Norwegian educational reform landscape up through the 1970s, remains Christie's only full-length engagement with the education system. Today, almost fifty years after the book was published in Norwegian, we are delighted to finally share Christie's profound perspectives on schools with a wider audience.

## A SOCIOLOGIST OF PROXIMITY

Unlike other prominent sociologists of the twentieth and twenty-first centuries—Jürgen Habermas, Anthony Giddens, Zygmunt Bauman, Ulrich Beck, and Hartmut Rosa—one will find no supertheory of modern, globalized societies and individuals in Christie's work. Christie's sociological perspective is always proximal: his focus is on agents who live in tangible structures, how they interact with these structures, and to what extent the structures prevent or promote possibilities for meaningful interactions with one's surroundings. Whether looking at the lives of criminalized Norwegian youths or misbehaving boys in the British school system, his work is characterized by an attention to how the frames *work*, so to say, on the lives, activities, and experiences of people. Christie's sociological starting point is the investigation of these dynamic frames, how they come about, and how those living in them might learn or see how to open them for change.

Christie's publications are filled with examples of how a careful sociological outlook may contribute to avail or create such openings. In Christie's seminal 1977 article in the *British Journal of Criminology*, "Conflicts as Property," it was exactly toward understanding and opening the "framework for conflict solution" that Christie directed his attention.[3] In the article, which would define the fields of criminology and restorative justice for many years, he denounces the supposed need for juridical specialists to handle the feelings, experiences, and relations of both offenders and victims caught in the system of law. In homogenizing and fixing these peoples' experiences, stories, and values within opaque procedures that relate far beyond the average capacities of ordinary people, Christie argues that "conflicts have been taken away from the parties directly involved and thereby have either disappeared or become other people's property."[4] Speaking from a communitarian point of view, this procedural disqualification of ordinary people's ability to participate in shared discussions of right or wrong risked paralyzing peoples' engagement in their environment. This is exactly, as made evident in this book, how specialized divisions of subjects and hierarchies in schools weaken the commitments of teachers, parents, school leaders, and students to nurture a vibrant school life that belongs to them and not to somebody else. Whether defending the right to experience and debate one's own conflicts or essential school activities, Christie was an unwavering advocate of the "pedagogical possibilities" of peoples' involvement in matters normally left to political or juridical authorities and professional institutions. His documentations of people struggling within bureaucratic frameworks are a testament to this "potential for activity [and] participation," which was, for Christie, an inherent aspect of people living and communicating together.[5]

## CHRISTIE'S SCHOOL

> If it is the case that we have set up society in such a way that there is no use for people in that society until they reach a certain age—and have chosen instead to gather them in institutions we have called schools—we should then direct our efforts toward converting these institutions into a type of miniature society where life can be lived to the fullest and in the most ordinary form as a matter of course. ... In our context, this means that the public school must first and foremost be a place to be, before it is a place to learn.

In the preface to *If Schools Didn't Exist*, Christie presents himself as an "outsider harboring few assumptions about schools." This is, of course, not entirely true. As Christie asserts, we all have expectations about what schools can and cannot achieve, for the simple reason that the majority of people in the world have spent a large bulk of their childhood grappling with reading, writing, algebra, and building friendships in them. Yet there is a different point to Christie's self-proclaimed distance. As some readers may be quick to observe in the absence of references to classical educational theorists, Christie refers above all to his distance from the

cultural and pedagogical conventions and programs undergirding the study of schools: educating for democracy (John
Dewey), educating for cognitive development (Jean Piaget),
educating for freedom (Jean-Jacques Rousseau), educating
for humanism (Carl Rogers), educating against oppression
(Paulo Freire), and so on. Aside from a critical comment on
the work of Ivan Illich, to whom Christie is often and somewhat mistakenly associated, no such references to educational theorists or movements appear in the book.[6] And as
Christie makes sure to emphasize, nor should they. *If Schools
Didn't Exist* is about schools in situ: concrete places with people operating within whichever framework they have been
provided. Christie proposes no canons, pedagogical principles, or organizational strategies for managing this operation
other than those he already knows of. But in not providing
this, he already offers a lot. *If Schools Didn't Exist* is a book
about how schools can become meaningful places to be—not
as society's de facto instrument of choice for realizing future
aspirations, but as organisms with lives of their own.

In Judith Suissa's introduction to the critical environment
of school research emerging at the time of Christie's writing, the highlighted similarities and differences between
Christie and his peers elegantly illustrate something of what
*If Schools Didn't Exist* has to offer. The premise of Christie's
contribution is, in fact, simple. Because we have structured
our societies around the need to ensure that knowledge and
forms of social organization are passed on from generation
to generation, the question is not *whether* schools are needed
but rather *how* they are needed. "If schools didn't exist" is, in
this paradoxical sense, a critical and impossible statement at
the same time. The school is here to stay as long as societies

exist—and exactly because of this, Christie accurately notes, the question of schools becomes a basic sociological problem. Under which conditions, he asks, can societies' "need to create formal routines that will attend to the needs of the coming generation" become meaningful? How can politicians, administrators, and other decision makers create frameworks to support the maintenance of this need in ways that does not paralyze those involved in the process? And who decides on behalf of our society the needs of the coming generation?

For Christie, inquiring into the life of the school is to inquire into the roots and core processes of society's way of coping with itself. Understanding Christie's school means understanding how this *coping* has been handled, how it is currently maintained, and how it could be improved in ways that better reflect the needs of the particular communities that the school serves. Going through the book's six chapters, we will briefly try to summarize and discuss why Christie's contribution is essential for anyone engaged or interested in such understanding—or perhaps, why they should be.

## THE SCHOOL IN SIX PARTS

In the opening chapter of the book, "Schools in Society: Three Case Studies," Christie presents three narrative examples of schools in different settings: the development of a French village school in the nineteenth century, the imposition of schools in the Sioux people's native community in the United States, and the stratified life of British lads attending the Lumley Secondary School in northern England. Each in their own way, he believes these examples are central to "acquire an experiential understanding of what makes a school a school."

The model of school that develops in Christie's account of the French village society during the nineteenth century is, uncoincidentally, the entry point for this analytic focus. As the villagers' lives were connected, both literally and figuratively, to goods, ideas, and roads reaching outside the village, they swiftly felt an increasing need for skills in arithmetic, reading, writing, and advanced knowledge about farming in order to communicate with and make use of the new possibilities. Even though the notion of a formalized school had come from the national government, the French village school, Christie argues, "first became relevant when changes in external factors clearly demonstrated a need for change in the inner structure," hereby becoming "a school in step with the requirements of a given era." Yet this sense of relevance is exactly what most school developers have forgotten. As Christie effectfully draws forth in recounting the stories of both the Sioux children and the lads attending Lumley Secondary School, the need for relevance in most societies has been replaced by an instrumental notion of schools as vehicles for socialization, assimilation, and the distribution of societal positions. By imposing standardized curriculums, teachers, and values whose necessities originate outside local communities, the schools of the Sioux people and British lads become *somebody else's school*—instruments to make the Sioux child think like an American and the British lad accept a hierarchical order in society.

But the aims, functions, and results of schools, Christie remarks, cannot exist or develop in isolation from their surroundings. Herein lies the perhaps most central point of the book's opening chapter: "once this system, which is called school, has been created, it attains a life of its own," taking form as "an organism that evolves in accordance with its own internal needs," which reflect the hierarchies and structures of the society that surrounds them. The Sioux child, it turns out, does not arrive as an empty room waiting to learn the language and values determined by politicians in Washington, DC. Nor does the British lad. Despite the intentions of those who seek to craft the school as an instrument for achieving specific purposes and promoting certain ways of acting, *children bring society with them into the school—and find, for good and bad, ways to live meaningfully on their own terms within the school's framework.* Asking what makes a school a school, then, means questioning the extent to which we as a society have provided a frame for children to experience themselves, their lives, and their communities as meaningful and relevant. In the French village school, this frame developed naturally. In our time, it is up to educators and politicians to ensure that such a frame exists.[7] There is, as the stories of the Sioux children and Lumley lads tragically confirm, everything at stake.

As schools have increasingly become instruments for external agendas, part of the difficulty in understanding them lies in their tendency to hold more than they promise. In the book's second and third chapters—"Social Order and the Reactions of Young People" and "If Schools Didn't Exist"—Christie introduces some of these central, albeit often-hidden instrumental needs that schools maintain. First is the school's function as a *storage space*. Children need a place to be while their parents work. In most contemporary societies, therefore, schools have come to serve as containers for the

segment of the unproductive population that cannot participate in the daily work routines of society—notably children
and teenagers, but as we see today, increasingly also adults.[8]
Second is what in most contemporary societies can be summarized as the need for *differentiation*. Society needs schools
to differentiate and allocate people based on merit to jobs
and further education. Without them, society would have no
way of determining who's successful and who's not, who's
talented and who's not. But as Christie has already demonstrated in chapter 1, schools are by no means isolated from
the social differences and social inequalities around them.
In effect, they do little except perpetuate the distributional
schemes within a seemingly meritocratic order.[9] A similar
logic runs through the third theme of Christie's critique—
namely, securing an adequate distribution of *knowledge*. In
our current situation, schools and similar institutions serve as
the only pathway to secure the transfer of knowledge within
society. Without schools, the learning required to function
in a specialized society with a constant growth of available
knowledge would cease or at least be heavily reduced, and for
this reason, schools as institutions of knowledge acquisition
are continuously legitimized. Yet for Christie, the purpose of
the school is not to create a *"knowledgeable* citizenry" for the
sake of knowing—we cannot know everything anyway—but
rather to provide a place where people are provided the tools
to look for themselves and figure out what they need to live
in a meaningful way. Similarly to the need for storage and
differentiation, the supposed necessity of institutionalized
knowledge transfer is based on a notion of the school as an
instrument for goals formulated outside the school.

In chapter 4, "Power in Schools," Christie delves deeper into the questions that follow from the previous chapter's investigations: Which mechanisms enable the school to function as an instrument reproducing the supposedly necessary functions of storage, differentiation, and knowledge transmission? And how, or in which type of societal framework, can the inner life of schools flourish? Once again, Christie does not look for answers to these questions in abstract principles or theoretical speculations. Through a thorough policy analysis of Norwegian parliamentary debates and reforms of the educational system from the nineteenth century up until the 1960s, he focuses instead on bringing to light the dual and opposing demands placed on schools from above. "On the one hand," Christie writes, "they [policy makers and educators] want to create a thriving school community, which is both beneficial and important. There is no cause to doubt the sincerity of their intentions in this regard. But they also want something else. They want to preserve the main characteristics of the existing organization of schools." Forced thus to achieve both ends at once, Christie brilliantly illustrates how politicians, school administrators, teachers, students, and subjects—despite the progressive aspirations across the board—remain bound to a mutual system of "hierarchically situated agencies" that "effectively remove[s] any form of sustenance for the inner life of schools." Teaching can occur only in allocated time slots. Learning is perceived only within the learning goals of the given subject. School budgets are correlated to the municipality's or state's regulations. For Christie, this situation is not the product of an inherently sluggish school bureaucracy but rather a society structured around specialization in tasks and knowledge that forces itself on the school's inhabitants. In this sense, any move toward a more vibrant and self-determining school does not imply that neither teachers nor school subjects should be banished or dissolved altogether. It is the ways in which "the inner life of schools parallels the common ways in which we organize ourselves" as a society of specialists and control that is at stake. What matters, in this sense, is that *what schools do* is accompanied by the structural support for teachers, students, and school principals to decide as well as reflect on for themselves *how to do it*, *who to manage it*, and *where it should lead*.

Chapter 5, "A Different School," merits the ambition of proposing how schools could develop and maintain the capacity to decide for themselves on the most important matters in school. Pivoting around the two central themes of *content* and *control*, Christie balances between installing and relinquishing determining factors that carve out his idea of schools—without becoming programmatic. The essential feature of the school in chapter 5, which is also the longest and arguably most central chapter of the book, is that of the school-society. Between the students, teachers, parents, and community members that comprise the school and its environment, the model of the school-society proposes a situation in which the school can decide for itself what and how the school should be, which factors its budgets should prioritize, and which positions its staff should occupy. In many ways, this notion of involvement mirrors Christie's defense of the "pedagogical possibilities" for victims, offenders, and laypeople to be involved in societal discussions of why we judge and punish as we do, as he proposed in "Conflicts as Property." Rather than leave aside such discussions to the idiosyncratic procedures and terms of specialists, Christie believed strongly in the societal benefits of people working out for themselves how to structure their everyday life. Why should schools have a budget at all if they could not decide what to do with it? If there is a shortage of benches in the schoolyard, one class may take the initiative to make benches for the school and learn about woodcraft. Some may paint the walls and learn about color. Some may stage a play, and learn about cooperation and drama. *School activities will always be different.* Similarly, what schools do will always depend on their location—the countryside evokes other possibilities than the city—just as the needs and aims of a given school's activities will be different due to the capabilities and values of that particular school-community. This is why standardization is not only a poor management strategy of schools; *it can never work.*

Importantly, Christie's call for self-determining institutions and locally sourced content does not imply that all parliamentary aspirations to create thriving school communities—and ensure some degree of uniform financial support—are a problem. Indeed, as inspiration, governmental or municipal support may be helpful and necessary for many schools, insofar as the decision-making capacities remain anchored in the local school. What matters, ultimately, is that each school is "granted dominion over its own life"—not in order to arrive at some grand educational program of freedom that Christie sees waiting on the horizon, but because the very procedures and disagreements of continuously arriving is integral for "learning to function as a community." In Christie's terms, the role of the government is to encourage these procedures, and especially to do so in spaces that lack resources for communal engagement. This is also why Christie, despite what many would find a logical extension of his previous arguments, did not support any movement to privatize schools, turn them into businesses, or introduce voucher programs based on the free choice of schools. His school is public—albeit perhaps not in the way that we are used to thinking about the term.

In chapter 6, "A Dream of a School," Christie unfolds a vision of society based on normalizing—and building our societal institutions around—the needs and values of local communities. In a fitting ending for a book that set out to explore social life, he guides the reader through a visit to a rural Camphill community in Norway, describing how school activities have been integrated into the heart of everyday life needs—cooking, cleaning, building sheds, singing, and reading.[10] Still today, the Camphill communities provide thousands of children and young adults with special needs a space to live, learn, and work together, representing what Christie believes to be an exemplary mode of noncategorizing engagement with people who, in many societies, would have been stowed away from communal activities. In a typical *Christie* fashion, there are no programmatic descriptions of a school-society but rather a careful portrait of a community in which people ordinarily considered disabled by society become "*able* within the framework that has been created."

The point of Christie's concluding depictions of the Camphill community should, by now, come as no surprise. By showing the benefits of constructing societal values, norms, practices, and culture around the actual experiential needs of people, Christie invites the reader to imagine a society where the means, materials, and categories for living are constantly debated as well as put into play, entangled with the realities in which they are embedded. Such a community is exactly what Christie seems to call for in the previous chapters' descriptions of the "inner life of schools." For good and bad, schools have a profound ability to reach beyond the formal frameworks that they have been given in most societies.

Although the majority of formalized school policies deny schools the possibility to become vibrant school-societies—by virtue of their preconceived normative aspirations and specialized systems—Christie does not give in to the temptation to do so. Nor would he, as current trends would have it, devolve the state's responsibility to private operators. Christie wants more, not less, school. But he wants it in a way that is *self-determining*. As in the French village detailed in the opening chapter of the book, Christie dreams of a school that will, once again, become the bedrock on which our societies rest—a proving ground for ways of living together in society. His school, then, is a society committed and trained to reflect—because the frameworks enable us to do so—"on how we want our lives to be, free from oppression, free to direct our society in relation to values that our schools had demonstrated were worthy of realization."

## THE PUBLIC LIFE OF SCHOOLS

The landscape of educational reform and thinking has naturally changed dramatically since *If Schools Didn't Exist* was published in 1971. From our first encounter with a torn paperback edition of the original text in summer 2014, the continued relevance of Christie's book has lingered in the back of our minds. Why should teachers, students, parents, and others interested in schools find it interesting to read a nearly half-century-old book written about an entirely different context? The easy answer to this question is to simply repeat what Christie himself, as he reflects on the need in most societies to standardize the routines and content of educating future generations, calls "the general problems at stake in the development of formal schooling." For Christie, these problems appear in any space that has decided to fulfill the apparent need for storage, differentiation, and knowledge distribution through its schools—and will continue to do so insofar as schools are considered necessary to maintain central aspects of societies around the world. In this sense, the stories of the French villagers, Sioux people, British lads, and Norwegian youths will be worth spending time understanding.

The second and perhaps less obvious answer follows as a corollary to the first. As noted above, much has changed since Christie and his peers documented the standardized forms of "banking education" that dominated in most industrialized societies during the 1960s and 1970s.[11] Somewhat paradoxically, the critique of formal schooling has since then become mainstream: from left to right on the political spectrum, schools have become symbols of a factory-like model of citizen-production that has no place in a dynamic and individualized learning economy. US secretary of education Betsy DeVos's repeated proclamation of "the public's awareness that traditional public schools are not succeeding" now figures as a mantra of many educational reforms across the world that seek to promote portfolios, Innovative

Learning Environments, e-learning, and other forms of individualized learning in their stead.[12] The positions have been reversed: as suggestions to substitute the school with "a learning environment that places the talents, choices and coaching needs of the learner first" have become ever-more normalized, growing numbers of scholars and politicians from both the radical Left and Right find themselves defending the school along with the authorities it has traditionally harbored.[13] And while the arguments in defense of the school vary—one preserving the need for institutionalized schools to bolster respect for traditional values, and the other shielding the school's institutionalized ability to neutralize the socioeconomic backgrounds of children, providing them with a shared space for learning that does not presuppose disparity—the ironic implication is hard to miss.[14] Can one propose an institutional critique of schools today without at the same time getting in bed with the neoliberal arguments propagated by DeVos and her colleagues, proposing to advance individual choice and competition between students and educational providers? Can one defend the school without concurrently preserving more or less conservative notions of universal content and authority that risks ignoring the school's surrounding communities as well as the cultural starting points of its inhabitants?

Fifty years on, we believe Christie's book can help us do exactly that. On the one hand, the mistrust of institutionalized schools for not accommodating individuals and their needs seems to resonate well with Christie's ambitions to root the school *within* society, and not behind barred gates. On the other hand, the belief in the unique possibilities to promote genuine opportunities for learning *in and through the school* is at the heart of Christie's project. It is exactly in proposing a dialectic between the self-determined inner life of schools and their surroundings that we are able to avoid the dead-ends noted above. Schools can and must work both *as societies, in society, and with the rest of the surrounding society*. And we need not look far to find possibilities for schools to do so—insofar as we, in recognizing the societal nature of schools, must at the same time come to terms with the fact that "no society can exist solely on the basis of the mutually provided services of its members." Christie writes,

> Is it not grotesque that nursing homes and schools, located across the street from each other, toil desperately away in isolation in their mutual and separate endeavors to solve opposite problems? Nursing homes are in need of nursing staff, and schools are in need of meaningful tasks for their students. ... Why shouldn't class 8B be responsible for doing the daily grocery shopping for the district's elderly residents who are living alone or stopping by on a regular basis to make sure everything is all right?

If considered on the basis of efficiently fulfilling the purportedly necessary tasks of the nursing home and school, the assigning of responsibility to the students of class 8B will probably fall short on many parameters. But then again, the widespread trend in social policies around the world to evaluate schools and other institutions according to efficiency in service delivery can hardly be perceived as a success, even in relation to the quality indicators that promoters of such policies propose.[15] In the words of educational philosopher Gert Biesta, the tendency to "displace the normative question of good education with technical and managerial questions about the efficiency and effectiveness of processes" has debased the engagement of teachers, students, and school leaders in the important deliberations about what they want as well as where they want to go.[16] In this sense, it is perhaps no surprise that a reorientation toward the pedagogical possibilities of such deliberations, defended so adamantly by Christie, seems to be coming back into fashion: citizens' councils, community building projects, and even partnerships between nursing homes and schools are popping up in many spaces.[17] Across these emerging projects is a recognition that treating tasks only as professional services ignores their potentials as interlocutors between the people who are involved and the society in which they take place. From involving children in painting a school's walls to getting acquainted with an inhabitant of a nursing home, a myriad of such possibilities are spread across the rugged surface of everyday life.

*If Schools Didn't Exist* is a testimony to the importance of these possibilities. Like a lung breathing in and breathing out, Christie reminds us that the school and its surrounding society are intricately connected. Both are vital for the other part to sustain itself—whether they like it or not.

## REFERENCES

Arriaga, Manuel. 2014. *Rebooting Democracy: A Citizen's Guide to Reinventing Politics*. London: Thistle Publishing.

Ball, Stephen. 2012. *Global Education Inc.: New Policy Networks and the Neo-Liberal Imaginary*. London: Routledge.

Biesta, Gert. 2010. *Good Education in an Age of Measurement: Ethics, Politics, Democracy*. London: Routledge.

Bloom, Allan. 1987. *The Closing of the American Mind*. New York: Simon and Schuster.

Bourdieu, Pierre, and Jean-Claude Passeron. 1977. *Reproduction in Education, Society and Culture*. London: Sage.

Bowles, Samuel, and Herbert Gintis. 1976. *Schooling in Capitalist America*. New York: Basic Books.

Christie, Nils. 1960. "Unge norske lovovertredere" [Young Norwegian law offenders]. PhD diss. Oslo University Press.

Christie, Nils. 1972. *Fangevoktere i konsentrasjonsleire* [Guards in concentration camps]. Oslo: Pax.

Christie, Nils. 1977. "Conflicts as Property." *British Journal of Criminology* 17 (1): 1–15.

Erickson, Megan. 2015. *Class War*. London: Verso.

Freire, Paulo. 1970. *Pedagogy of the Oppressed*. London: Continuum.

Gadotti, Moacir, and Carlos Alberto Torres. 2009. "Paulo Freire: Education for Development." *Development and Change* 40 (6): 1255–1267.

Illich, Ivan. 1971. *Deschooling Society*. New York: Harper and Row.

Larsen, Steen Nepper. 2019. "Blindness in Seeing: A Philosophical Critique of the Visible Learning Paradigm in Education." *Education Sciences* 9 (1): 1–12.

Lomell, Heidi Mork, and Vidar Halvorsen. 2015. "Nils Christie, 1928–2015." *Journal of Scandinavian Studies in Criminology and Crime Prevention* 16 (2): 142–144.

Masschelein, Jan, and Maarten Simons. 2014. *In Defense of the School: A Public Issue*. Leuven: Education, Culture and Society Publishers.

*Philanthropy*. 2013. "Interview with Betsy DeVos, the Reformer." Spring. https://www.philanthropyroundtable.org/philanthropy-magazine/article/spring-2013-interview-with-betsy-devos-the-reformer.

Rancière, Jacques. 1991. *The Ignorant Schoolmaster: Five Lessons in Intellectual Emancipation*. Stanford, CA: Stanford University Press.

Srnicek, Nick, and Alex Williams. 2016. *Inventing the Future*. London: Verso.

# EDITORS'
# ACKNOWLEDGMENTS

There are many people—too many to mention here—to whom we are thankful for helping us bring *If Schools Didn't Exist* into contact with a wider audience. Much like Christie's model of the school-society developing as an organism to attain a life of its own, the process of translating and editing has generated discussions and new acquaintances that have all contributed to convince us of the relevance as well as importance of sharing the work at this moment in time. We are grateful to the people who were involved, each in their own way, either at some point or throughout the journey. They include our editor at the MIT Press, Susan Buckley, whose skillful facilitation and helpful comments have been invaluable throughout the process; Judith Suissa for ongoing dialogues and reflections, and elegantly situating and bringing to life the book's continued significance; Peter Plant for pointing us toward the book in early spring 2014; Hedda Giertsen and Pål Frogner for helping us get closer to the context of Christie's life and work; Diane Oatley for thoughtful feedback and revisions of the manuscript; Louise Cone and Tora Frogner for precious clarifications and comments throughout the work of translation and editing; Steen Nepper Larsen for feedback and ongoing conversations on the book's arguments within a contemporary context; Norwegian Literature Abroad for supporting the translation; and finally, Olivia and Tora for supporting both our hearts and minds while going at it.

# PREFACE

Schools are like radars. Through them we can discern the nature of our society. At the same time, we can apply other types of knowledge about that society in an effort to understand why our schools have acquired their current form.

It is important to understand our schools. They represent nine years of life for all of us, and twelve to fifteen years for many. Schools are marked by the surrounding society, but also leave their mark on us. This makes it necessary to acquire an experiential understanding of what makes a school a school. This is the underlying motivation of this book.

The book will have many shortcomings. If I have but one advantage in writing about this theme, it is that of being an outsider harboring few assumptions about schools. Yet this will also increase the chances of losing my way. There is certainly a great deal that has not been accurately perceived, and educationists might have expressed themselves in stronger terms. In this context, there is one thing that I hope some readers will keep in mind: this is not a book about teachers.

Nor is it a book about students. This is a book about social life. I have a strongly held belief that most people do the best they can within the framework of their social circumstances. It is the framework that interests me, and only parts of the framework. There is no need to repeat what is commonly said about schools.

For that reason, much more could have been said in each section of this book; arguments and counterarguments could have been raised, and conclusions drawn, about the doubt-fulness of the case I am making. These deliberations have been left out. Readers are free to entertain any such doubts as they see fit. I have tried to carve out a whole. Polishing may hinder contact with the object. I have something important to say. And I want to say it now.

—*Nils Christie*
*Oslo, September 1971*

P.S. Many people deserve thanks, in particular the commu-nity at the Institute for Criminology and Criminal Law. Nev-ertheless, there is no one from whom I have learned more than Lindis Charlotte and Anja Catharina. For that reason, I extend a special thank you to them as well.

# 1

## SCHOOLS IN SOCIETY: THREE CASE STUDIES

It is often easier to move forward by way of a short detour. In this chapter, I will present some of the books and studies that have influenced and inspired me. The selection may seem arbitrary and confusing, but I would ask the reader not to despair. The studies I present below have an inherent value. But more important, as will be demonstrated in the following chapters, the combined studies illustrate the underlying premise of the main ideas presented in this book.

### A FRENCH VILLAGE

If you take the train from Paris to Bordeaux, and a slow, meandering train at that—a train that stops at points of local interest along the way—after a while you will reach a tiny station located near a tiny village. Mazières-en-Gâtine is the name of the village, and Roger Thabault (1971) is the name of the man who has described it.[1] Both names are worth noting. For although the village remains minuscule and Thabault is now an old man, I feel certain that the book he wrote about the village of his childhood will remain a monument in the history of public education. This point is even more remarkable considering that Thabault writes very little about schools or education in the book.

What he does write a good deal about is the village itself. The name of the village, Mazières-en-Gâtine, indicates that it was probably built in the vicinity or on top of ancient Roman ruins. It was far from an attractive building site. An abundance of natural wells and water holes were the only local resources that could help explain the decision to choose to build a village in precisely this location. In the years around 1750, water was thus the only immediately available resource for the hundreds of households located in and around the village. Most of the inhabitants were tenants and bond servants who fought a desperate battle on infertile soil against weeds, water, fog, and landowners—and not least the French military service that recruited soldiers to take part in the glorious military adventures of the fatherland. The population's garments were simple, hand sewn, and made of hemp. And if people were lucky enough to have shoes, these were carved out of wood. The wealthier residents had one set of clothes made of wool that was intended to last for a lifetime. The food was, of course, homegrown and home cooked. Salt, pepper, and candles were the only commodities imported into the village on a regular basis. Wine was a luxury enjoyed by only the wealthiest members of the population. All tools were handmade, including the wooden plow. The crude plow blade would scratch at the surface of the soil, with the sole advantage being that the plow itself could be drawn by even the most decrepit of livestock. The houses had just one room; animals huddled in one corner, a kitchen was found in the second, and beds in the third. It was an existence rife with hunger, illness, frostbite, and destitution, and for a long time these conditions remained unchanged. In 1855, the population was around 970. Out of these, 159 were dependent on public welfare to survive the coldest and most difficult years.

Settlement was dispersed, and in 1840, less than 200 of the township residents lived in the actual village. Most were craftspeople who farmed on the side, but two or three landed proprietors, along with a priest, doctor—uneducated, naturally—tax collector, teacher, and four police officers also lived in the village.

We will soon learn more about the teacher. But before that, a few words about the road builder, because he is the first to make an entrance in the lifeworld that Thabault describes. The road builder arrived in 1850. Before that time, and for a long time afterward, travel was a perilous undertaking. In the words of Thabault (1971, 42),

> It is possible to gain an idea of what the roads were like at the time simply by looking at the plowing tracks in a field. Just a couple of inches below the surface, there is an impenetrable layer of sediment, leading to flooded roads with every rainfall. Thick hedges protect the roads from the sun. They are almost constantly muddy, even during the summer, and most of the time completely impassable. Passage is possible only by oxcart, as persons traveling on foot will find themselves ankle deep in the mud. The conditions were even worse before 1850 due to the bushes and heather invading the road. And as if that were not enough, Baron de Tusseau had only to relocate a fence and the road would become a part of his outlying fields.
>
> In year IX following the revolution, Prefect Dupin wrote, "The roads of Gâtine are passable only toward the end of summer, and on the ridges the roads are blocked by large stones

that can be removed only by blasting with dynamite. In the road there are many deep craters filled with mud, which are covered by a thin layer of dry soil. The horses traveling there fall through, and several oxen are needed to haul them out again.

On the whole, it was, still in the words of Thabault, a closed world. There were few who traveled. Everyone knew a little about everything and had no need to go anywhere. Every once in a while, a villager would venture to a local market in the neighboring village, but for the majority, the weekly expedition to church every Sunday was enough. No one left, and no one arrived. The first records of birthplaces in the township appeared in 1872, and showed that only five people were born outside the county and eighteen were born in neighboring townships. Only the most important of dignitaries enjoyed a slightly larger network of contacts. A messenger brought them letters on a weekly basis, but due to the small amount of mail in and out of the village, the messenger was not entitled to the use of a horse.

There was a school in the village. Here is its birth certificate:

Today, on June 10, 1832, the undersigned members of the village council in Mazières have gathered for an extraordinary meeting to address the circular letter of May 17 … regarding funds for a primary school teacher.

Given that the township has never before had a teacher or even a building to teach in, but at the same time wholly acknowledges the pressing need for procuring such a teacher— the village council unanimously agrees to the approval of a surtax of sixty francs to provide the teacher with a salary and will submit a request to the government—as the surtax will surely be insufficient—that it supply whatever outstanding amount might be necessary to employ a teacher. (Thabault 1971, 52)

The initiative for the school came from Paris. Mazières was one of the few townships that welcomed the idea. The surrounding townships either dismissed it out of hand or remained skeptical. As became quickly apparent, it was difficult to find support for this new idea of a school. Teachers came, but soon left again. They were offered extremely primitive conditions. And most important, they were given no children to teach.

The thoughts of the politicians in Paris were as follows:

Make no mistake: while the teacher's profession may be without glamor, and his daily duties confined within the borders of a single township, his work is of importance to the entire society. His profession represents an invaluable contribution to public life. It is not just for the sake of the township's welfare or out of consideration for mere local interests that the law requires that all Frenchmen—if possible—acquire the necessary skills deemed indispensable for social life and intelligent behavior. It is also for the sake of both the state and public interests: freedom can only flourish among people who are sufficiently enlightened as to be able to attend the voice of reason. A common and compulsory education for all will henceforth guarantee order and stability in our society. Because our country is governed by the pillars of truth and rationality, it is only through the development of intelligence and enlightenment that we may secure the continuance of the constitutional monarchy. (François Guizot, quoted in Thabault 1971, 56–57)

These notions were conceived in Paris. But the children of Mazières lived on dirt floors, waded through mud, and lived their lives primarily within the closed circle of their community. They needed to be able to perform basic calculations—a skill most of the children either learned by themselves or from each other. Yet all the other stuff from Paris, which was to be taught in the classroom, was alien and above all useless.

Advanced numeracy was unnecessary—the household economy was based on the simple barter and trade of natural goods. Public announcements and official news were communicated by word of mouth. What was most important was the local news, and no schooling was required for the oral manner of its communication. The village church, fireplace, and water pump all retained their double functions.

But then the road builder arrived and began his work in 1848. Most of the roads were completed in seven years' time. The first railroad tracks arrived twenty years later. The bubble had finally burst. Only then did the school find its true meaning.

Studies show for whom the school was important during the first years of its existence. Village residents were the first to recognize the need for schooling. The baker's balance sheets became too complex to calculate accurately through simple mental arithmetic, and the blacksmith acquired a need for new materials from outside the village. So they sent their sons to school. A post office soon followed. More than anyone, the postmaster depended on the written word, and reading soon became a general requirement—even for girls. The village slowly grew in size—from 200 inhabitants in 1850 to 250 in 1870—and more craftspeople arrived: cobblers, clockmakers, and fabric and yarn dyers. The documented arrival of craftsmen and artisans indicates that something must have happened in the village. The villagers were now able to afford new shoes and watches. They also started dying their clothes. The road was opened; products were sent out, and money and new impulses came in. And little by little, the farm children started appearing in the school statistics, at first only boys, but soon also girls.

Soon the farmers were able to avail themselves of yet another opportunity: in 1849, an agricultural school was founded near the village. Apparently the founding of this school occurred purely by chance. One of the larger landed proprietors owned several fertile farms along with one that was extremely infertile, which he turned over to the government in exchange for the establishment of an agricultural school, where he would hold a paid post of director. The school targeted farmers from a large area, and the teachings were quite abstract. The local farmers had no use for it—on the contrary, they became angry and demanded that a research commission from the government conduct a review of the school. Teach farming—at a school? Never! But with time, the crops in the area began to flourish. One neighbor took a leap of faith and bought himself an iron plow identical to the one used at the college. And although the local farmers had distanced themselves from the school, they flocked around the neighbor: the first time he put the plow to use, more than 200 people came to watch. Curiosity notwithstanding, they remained unconvinced. The plow dug too deeply and was criticized for unearthing the infertile soil lying underneath the good soil. But when the time for harvest came, the man with the iron plow brought in abundant crops. The plow had uprooted the nightmarish weeds, and the following year, many iron plows could be seen in the fields. The development of new fertilization methods soon followed, along with the introduction of different types of grain, and more than ever, the road and railroad were needed to deal with the unprecedented surplus. In fact, no column of

**Table 1.1** Transported Goods to and from Mazières between 1885 and 1910

|        | Express trains      |                     | Slow trains         |                     |
|--------|---------------------|---------------------|---------------------|---------------------|
| Year   | Export in tons      | Import in tons      | Export in tons      | Import in tons      |
| 1885   | 6                   | –                   | 1,208               | 2,482               |
| 1890   | 33                  | –                   | 1,405               | 4,312               |
| 1900   | 181                 | 77                  | 2,304               | 4,807               |
| 1910   | 324                 | 83                  | 2,867               | 6,195               |

*Source*: Thabault 1971, 145.

numbers is more suitable to start this book than that found in table 1.1, showing the village's statistics for outgoing and incoming goods by rail between 1885 and 1910. The increasing necessity of the village school is reflected in this table.

There were other reasons as well. Compulsory military service was introduced, and young men were to a much greater extent obliged to leave the confines of the village. Asking your friend to write the letter home to your girlfriend—or knowing that it would be read aloud to her by a friend— was an unpleasant prospect. It was not only the effects of one iron plow that could be clearly discerned: the benefits of schooling for the first students also became increasingly evident. Some of the township's poorest children, who were not needed at home, were therefore among the first to attend the school. These children finished school at the same time as the village opened up to the outside world, and suddenly a large number of jobs—and from a farmer's perspective, attractive jobs—materialized. The poor lad with an education sailed straight past the others. Later, other children from more affluent families also found themselves with more free time on their hands and were sent to school as well. As machines began to take over, children were no longer needed at home to the same extent, and schooling soon became a matter of course. We will return to this subject in another chapter.[2]

On top of this, critical events were also unfolding in France. Kings came and kings went—mostly the latter. New forms of governance emerged. Without roads, none of this would have mattered. Norwegian officials were probably better informed of events in Paris than the average citizen of Mazières. But the roads and railroad brought more than just goods and money; they brought new ideas as well. Landowners slowly lost their monopoly on important decisions about community matters. Local opposition emerged in keeping with national trends. There was a fireworks display on the day of the Republican victory in the local elections. And soon enough, the information shared at the village water pump became insufficient. Newspapers began arriving—sent free of charge to the most influential citizens in the village. Those who could not read were excluded from all this.

The changes in Mazières spelled trouble for the village priest. Others, too, were now able to read, and suddenly the roads began leading to places other than heaven. Three central movements emerged that would replace religion: nationalism, republicanism, and—as the ultimate driving force—the belief in progress. Or rather, the certitude of progress—progress leading the village residents out of hardship, destitution, and disenfranchisement into an existence of waving fields of grain, prosperity, and dignity. The road had become an integrated part of the village, and for generation after generation, the school was seen as the key to all this. The school became the bedrock on which everything else rested.

## THE EMPTY ROOMS

A dreary landscape. Dusty roads, randomly situated wood shacks, a number of tents. Forty thousand people. And there, towering behind it all like a temple, the school.

We are in Dakota, United States.[3] The home of many of Norway's destitute—farm boys without an allodial entitlement, children of smallholders, and the impoverished, along with the occasional black sheep who made the journey in hopes of changing the color of his fleece "over there." The landscape was vast, open, and uninhabited.

Well, almost uninhabited. The unlucky groups of people that were already settled on the land were quickly driven out and subsequently resettled on tracts of uncultivable land, such as the Pine Ridge district. Here the Sioux people were given new land—or old sand.[4]

They were doing fine, if by doing fine we mean to say they were not starving. Their former hunting grounds were being cultivated by the Scandinavian farmers. There was surplus produce, the conditions for trade were difficult, and Sitting Bull and One Feather received weekly deliveries free of charge. There were plenty of old clothes. No starvation, no nudity.

But becoming American—in the sense of European—was not in the cards for them. The common wisdom of the time was that if you give them money, they will drink it up, and waste their time on tomfoolery or shooting the breeze or just staring up at the clouds.

The nights were still spent doing the old ritual dances. Living conditions remained far removed from the American dream: water was taken from the brook, heat was provided by a fireplace, and the water closet was at best an outhouse. Even their language was kept alive: in Pine Ridge, most people spoke the "L" dialect of the Dakota language—that is, Lakotan. Only those living near the main roads spoke English, along with a few of those living a bit further away, but mostly there were many who merely pretended to do so. On the outskirts of the district, an interpreter was required. The word "interpreter," by the way, also means "half-breed" in the Lakota language. If anything, this illustrates how during those early years, so few Europeans lived in the region that they coexisted—mostly in peace—with the native population.

And now to the schools. A group of federal schools was built in the region, funded by Washington, DC. Amends were to be made for past injustices; the schools were built and equipped to offer the Native American children the same satisfactory educational standards as those offered to the rest of the country. Solid, modern buildings, fully equipped classrooms, cafeterias, running water, and working toilets. Three to four buses collected the children every day from even the remotest of locations, the youngest were given breakfast at school, and all the children received lunch. A staff of qualified teachers was ready and waiting, eager to fill up the day as well as the children.

In spite of these measures, or perhaps exactly because of them, things went terribly wrong. The results from the primary schools were among the lowest 10 percent in the country, and did not even include the large number of children who dropped out of school completely and made up about half of an average class. Of the few who made it to high school, only one out of three students completed their studies—once again with dreadful results. This third of the students also included quite a large group of children whose parents were teachers or state employees on the reservation. *Why did things go so wrong?* The answer to this question is explained in a study dear to my heart. It was cowritten by a number of authors, all of whom deserve mention: Murray L. Wax, Rosalie H. Wax, and Robert V. Dumont Jr., assisted by Rosely Holyrock and Gerald OneFeather. Henceforth, reference to the study will be Wax, Wax, and Dumont 1964).

In the study of why things went so dreadfully wrong for the Pine Ridge people, three elements in particular stand out. First, it was a school *based on a vacuum theory*. It hereby became a *degrading school*. And it became an *irrelevant school*. Other readers will perhaps highlight other important aspects of the study. The authors offer examples of extreme incompetence on the part of school personnel as a critical contributing factor. But such factors are not of interest, unless there is a frequency indicating that they represent a trend. As is the case for most other social schemes, we must assume schools to be staffed with average personnel. Some are extremely competent, and others are extremely incompetent, but the majority are average. The system must be designed in terms of the average. If "the average" cannot be used, another kind of system must be created.

As we were saying, the teachers were there, prepared to fill up both the day and the children. Hidden in this formulation lies the key to understanding *the vacuum theory*. We could have given it another name: the blotting paper ideology. Or the theory of the empty rooms. Or tabula rasa. The point is that the student is regarded as someone who is completely empty when meeting the teacher—or at best, unfortunate enough to be burdened with irrelevant or unwanted prior knowledge. In the words of two distinguished administrators,

> This kid from a conservative home began attending the school. He only speaks his Native American tongue; everything he knows comes from his grandmother's teachings. His home has no books, no magazines, no radio, no television. And then he goes to school, and we have to teach him everything. OK, so we bring him to the point where he actually knows a little about something, and then he drops out of school. Our numbers are high for kids like that—who drop out before completing their final exams. The reason is simply that at some point, he is forced to choose between his grandmother and becoming an educated person. ... If only we had reached the child earlier, maybe at kindergarten or nursery school age—we should have a nursery here—then we could have achieved more with the kid.

Or as another administrator puts it,

> The Native American child has such a limited horizon. Ask him to read words like "elevator" or "escalator," and he will have no idea what the words mean. But the issue lies not only with foreign words or concepts. Take a word such as "water." When you or I think of it, well, we think of stainless steel, running water, a shiny sink—pure, clean water—and the pipes that supply it, sewers, purification plants, and the half-million-dollar water supply project for the Pine Ridge area. But the Native American child doesn't exactly think of water as something flowing into a bathtub. (Quoted in Wax, Wax, and Dumont 1964, 67–68)

Wax, Wax, and Dumont (1964, 68) comment that "while he [the administrator] was talking, we thought about our camping trip last summer by the small river just a couple of hundred meters away from the Sioux settlement. We recalled the cool water, the vegetation around it, and the people coming to bathe along with their animals."

In their ignorance, the administrators' utterances sound like such a caricature that I was hesitant to cite them here. That is, until I found myself in lecture hall five, eagerly teaching a group of zealous Norwegian students about different forms of social control. First I spoke at great length about complex theories. Then I tried starting a conversation. Vacant gazes stared back at me. These students had just commenced their studies. They couldn't be expected to participate in something like this. One of them even got angry with me. They were here to *learn*. Not to be put on display in all their ignorance. How were they supposed to know how people control one another? He was right. I had alienated the content and begun at the (wrong) end of a complex theory, where none of my students had been before. Suddenly, not a single one of the students knew a single thing about something they did every day: the ways in which they encourage, curb, control, and direct one another. The vacuum theory had implicitly prevailed. It was not the first time and it will certainly not be the last.

But some cases are, of course, more extreme than others. These cases occur especially in situations where the greatest distance exists between the current or prospective lives of the pupils and teachers. The gap between the Sioux people and their teachers was insurmountable. The teachers resided in quaint detached houses, located near the area of the school.

Their working day was long, but in their leisure time, they could do as they pleased. Traveling within the district, however, was difficult. There were no road signs, and no numbers on the houses—local familiarity with the district alone was helpful. Add to this the language barriers, and uncertainty as to whether or not they were even welcome in the Sioux territory, and the gap widens. Only a single teacher went on regular visits to their hometown.

The school thereby became the disseminator of all the things that the Native Americans were lacking: how to use the toilet, how to eat a hamburger properly, how to be polite to adults, and all the other *things* and *symbols* that were supposedly important outside their community.

Naturally, a gap between the teacher and student is not unique to this case. This distance is the norm. Two peers have little to learn from each other. One of them must know something that the other doesn't.

In some cases, the vacuum theory might even be fully acceptable—it might even be the best foundation for learning. These are cases in which the theory provides an accurate description of the situation, whereby it is acceptable for the students, and their acceptance provides the students with subsequent benefits. The example of Asian university students seeking to learn how to speak Norwegian in Norway is useful here. It seems fair to assume that the students will know nothing, and that the "rooms" must be filled. This premise alone makes initial failure acceptable for both students and teachers, while at the same time making any later achievements seem all the more glorious.

But then there are many cases in which such premises are flawed. In these cases, it is first and foremost the refusal to base the teaching on what the students already know that is pedagogically unsound. This point is basic. Yet on top of this, although it might be a bit more difficult to understand, comes the implication of the theory of the empty rooms—which are in no sense empty—and entails that whatever was in the room to begin with must be pushed aside. The teacher stomps blindly into the classroom, doing their best to fill up the rooms on top of all the things that are already in there, but that they cannot see. Perhaps some of the existing contents are shoved out during the process, some are broken, while other contents may be sturdy enough to circumvent the teacher's attempts to shove them away or even replace them. *In every case, the teacher's conduct inevitably leads to an understanding among the students that whatever was in the room wasn't worth having there in the first place.*

This describes the situation in Pine Ridge. The vacuum theory resulted in *a degrading school*. The ideals of the white man found expression in the white man's books, even more so in his behavior, and most of all in his things. And of all the white man's things, nothing was more important and more removed from reality than the school itself. Previously, the Sioux people's schools had been small and scattered throughout the district until they were combined into a single, central school. "The Native Americans' own school," they called it on its opening day. This claim did not last long after the school was asked to host a "native gathering." Dirt, rowdiness, and disorder followed—once was more than enough. Such things have no place in what was, clearly, the white headmaster's school. Parents brought their children to school on their first day. They rarely stepped onto the school grounds again. Everything was set up in a way that facilitated the experience of inferiority. And like my Norwegian students, the Sioux parents reacted by avoiding situations of degradation as much as they could.

The children followed the parents' lead. This is the crucial point in the analysis provided by Wax and his colleagues. While their point is especially significant in the case of the Sioux people, its features are to be found in other cultures as well. The Sioux have a deep-rooted belief in human beings as fundamentally stable. The joyful person will almost always be joyful, the kind person always kind, and the foolish person always foolish. This makes it all the more important *not* to be made a fool of. All reasonable members of the tribe know this, and arrange their lives accordingly. When mistakes are made, great efforts are made to cover them up. And when there is a need to correct someone's behavior, much care is taken to ensure that this takes place in private and the dignity of both parties is preserved.

But the theory of the empty rooms leaves little room for dignity. The teacher's persona and ideals imply that the student is inherently inferior—a fact that is highlighted in the classroom situation. Here, the young Sioux is put in situations where they will inevitably do everything wrong. They will make a fool of themselves in public, be corrected in public, and on top of it all, be told to respect and cooperate with the person whom, little by little, is experienced as an intruder in the room that is already filled to the brim.

For the child or young person, this is unavoidable. School attendance is compulsory, and most parents genuinely believe that schooling must somehow be good for the child. Besides, the school provides free lunch, among others things. As for the school, it is granted a certain amount of money per child, and consequently the bar for expulsion is pretty high. But dignity is more important than food. The result is physical attendance, but mental absence.

This is not, however, the case in the earliest years of schooling. Eager children attend willingly, doing their best to understand some of the strange words coming out of the strange person's mouth. They're too young to have any dignity to lose and too excited about the unknown. But before long, two things start to happen. First, protests. Chaos erupts in the classroom, especially among children who tease or bully one another. This is a recurring theme in teachers' complaints about the Native American schools: the children harass one another constantly and do so with an unbridled vengeance. The explanation for this phenomenon is multifaceted. Most of the children are used to living in small neighborhood communities where hierarchies are established quickly, and peace and order prevail. But in the centralized school, all these power relations must be tested anew. The children are accustomed to equality between people and inequality in age, which enables the elders to protect the young members of the community. In school, the opposite occurs: there is inequality between the children and equality in age. At home, the adults serve as courts of appeal in the event somebody should cross over the line too frequently. But at school, the only adult person present is the representative of the empty rooms—the person who must be avoided at all costs. And so the children are left to manage things on their own. The first couple of years become nightmarish.

And yet they pull through. In the end, they manage to establish some form of stable, hierarchical order. By seventh and eighth grade, order and silence prevail. The only sounds being made are coming from the teacher. The students are as unresponsive as mollusks:

> Hours pass without a single word being uttered by any student. The incredible discipline ruling the upper classes is created and enforced by the Sioux children themselves in relation to both teachers and peers. Their self-imposed discipline serves as a shield. Behind it, unprepared or unwilling students can hide, turning most teachers into useless or ridiculous figures, and for the first time in many years, the students find themselves in a calm and orderly environment. Here, they are allowed to daydream, pass each other notes, read books from the library, and even study if they wish to do so. The only disturbance is the teacher's voice, but they have nonetheless long since learned how to tune in and out, according to their own needs and inclinations. The teachers usually react to this in one of three different ways. Some resign themselves to the silence as if it were inevitable, allowing it to prevail and instead working individually with those of the children who seem willing to cooperate. Some go to great lengths to keep talking, indifferent to any response or lack thereof from the pupils. And finally, at its most extreme and in clear contrast to Sioux customs, some teachers shake and terrorize their students to force a mechanical reply out of them, or simply frighten the children so they stop coming to school altogether. (Wax, Wax, and Dumont 1964, 98)

The observers of these classes provide accounts of how the teachers, in one way or another, make pathetic attempts to penetrate the shield. They force answers out of the students, pretend to hear the answers they hope for, or try to read the answers from facial expressions or body postures. Of equal cause for concern are the responses of the students. In the event of direct confrontations, the offending student will duck under the lid of their desk, pretend not to have heard, and look in totally a different direction or feign stupidity. For them, any one of these responses is better than answering,

better than making a fool of themselves, or better than showing signs of a willingness to cooperate with the person who
does not accept the students in the first place.

Under such circumstances, it is clear that little learning
takes place in the school. The issue of an extreme *lack of relevance*, constituted by both external and internal conditions,
is another part of this equation. The external conditions are
tied closely to the state of Dakota in the 1960s. Most of the
fertile lands for farming are controlled by white men. Few are
able to coax any form of crops out of the sandy fields left for
the Sioux people. Table 1.2 illustrates the working situation
of fathers of the Sioux families in Pine Ridge.

**Table 1.2** Occupational Distribution of Family Fathers of the Pine
Ridge Sioux People

|  | Quantity | Percentage |
|---|---|---|
| Agriculture | 557 | 21.4 |
| Unskilled | 136 | 5.2 |
| State employed | 129 | 5.0 |
| Military | 120 | 4.6 |
| Skilled or semiskilled | 101 | 3.9 |
| Service sector | 44 | 1.7 |
| Supervisors | 28 | 1.1 |
| "Tribal" workers | 26 | 1.0 |
| Unemployed | 1,379 | 52.9 |
| No information | 86 | 3.3 |
|  | 2,606 | 100.0 |

*Source*: Wax, Wax, and Dumont 1964, 23.

More than half are unemployed, and only one-fifth have managed to find employment in agriculture. Of those who have, the majority are half-breeds—in other words, "almost" white. More than half of all the families' annual incomes are less than a thousand dollars per year, at a time when a mere 15 percent of the total population of Dakota had such a low income. And again, a large portion of this 15 percent in Dakota as a whole were without doubt Native American. Such are the circumstances for the Sioux students, of the life to which they will return. It is far from self-evident how a national curriculum with a standardized view of achievement might have any kind of impact in such a context.[5]

Only under one condition would the Sioux people's school become relevant: if life were to be lived off the reservation. But here, the internal conditions of the school come into play. The students know very well that they are not learning anything at school. They experience it themselves and see it in their fellow tribesmen, none of whom have been equipped with the intellectual or practical prerequisites that would enable them to leave the reservation. Knowing this, schooling becomes even more irrelevant and the students even less inclined to learn. The vicious circle tightens its grip. That is, of course, *if* it is considered vicious in the first place by the reservation. After all, the latter retains its people—also the best ones.

## THE CENTRIFUGE

"Lumley" Secondary School is located somewhere in the heart of northern England. The name and location of the school are fictitious. In reading the following, the necessity of such camouflaging will eventually become evident.

Two young lads, two worlds, and one school. Or should they in fact be considered *two* schools? On the contrary, as it is precisely because they have been forced to attend the same school that two separate worlds have been created. David Hargreaves (1967) illustrates this clearly. Adrian and Clint would probably not be as fully Adrian and Clint were it not for the fact that for four years, they were forced into a confrontation with each other, their fellow students, and their teachers—and above all with their own self-image as reflected in all these encounters.

It all takes place somewhere in northern England. A dirty, industrial town of dreary houses, but often inhabited by warmhearted individuals. The school is only ten years old, but it too is already shrouded in an aura of grayness. Four hundred and fifty students, most of them from working-class families, absorb the knowledge dispensed by the twenty-four teachers employed at the school. Only a single teacher lives in the school neighborhood. The majority of the others live in a residential district outside the town's limits. At the lower secondary school, the students are given four years of schooling from the age of twelve to fifteen. At that point they also have the option of continuing for an additional, noncompulsory fifth year.

Adrian and Clint began in the same class. Both had done well on their primary school leaving exams and therefore were naturally placed in the A-level class—the best class out of the school's four levels.[6] The school's level division is without any pretension of equality among the students. The level divisions are categorized alphabetically. Smart students are put in the A level, and the incorrigible are placed in the B level. And what's more, the school even has an E level for those so far removed from the school society that Hargreaves himself chose not to include this class in his investigation. This choice is one of the few weaknesses of his study.

So Adrian and Clint began in the same class with somewhat similar prerequisites for learning. But then something happened to Clint. The triggering incident remains unknown. Yet the result of his transformation is conveyed through several sources. During an audiotaped interview, one of Clint's former classmates explains it as follows:

> In 1B I used to hang out with Clint. He was all right. He is sensible when you're alone with him. He's smart. He could have been good at sports and all that, but he just refused to take the class. It's the teachers' fault really. Cause he was in 1A. But because he misbehaved, they sent him down to 1E. If they'd kept him in the A-level class, he could have been cock of the roost by now. (Quoted in Hargreaves 1967, 120)

Described in more detail, Clint's development was as follows: Clint comes afoul of his homeroom teacher during his first year of school. As a form of shock treatment in punishment for his behavior, he is transferred temporarily to the E-level class. He is then allowed to return, albeit not to the A-level class. Instead he is delegated to the B level, where he must prove himself once more. But from here on in, his performance in school rapidly deteriorates. From being second best in his B-level class he descends first down to number six, then twenty-first, and then finally ending at thirty. And that is the total number of students in the class. He is then transferred to the C-level class, where he ends up as number twenty-one out of twenty-three. And then lower secondary school comes to an end.

It is difficult to find an explanation for this development. Hargreaves holds that it was because Clint made friends in the C- and D-level classes, and thereby was motivated to work his way down to their level. But why didn't he make friends with his A-level classmates instead? Perhaps he was on bad terms with some of the students in the A-level class. Perhaps there was not enough room for both him and Adrian. This remains unanswered. All we know for certain is that as Clint descended on the ladder of achievement, he became the natural leader of the C- and D-level classes due to his intellectual abilities (and physique).

Viewing this development from the outside, Clint and Adrian became kings of their own kingdoms. First Adrian— neatly groomed and well dressed, the school's most trusted representative, the undisputed leader of his class, one of the best students at the school, with almost perfect attendance, positive in his attitude, but also clear about his requirements for effective instruction on the part of the teachers. And then Clint—long, unkempt hair and working hard every day to keep it that way, dressed in blue jeans, a violation of the school dress code, known as the school brawler, liked by some, obeyed by many, a high level of absenteeism, considered a scourge by the teachers, and wishing for nothing else but the duress of school to soon come to an end.

We can imagine the kind of answer that Clint would give to describe his dream of adult life:

*What do you most look forward to doing when you finish school?*

*Strolling around at home with a cigarette butt in my mouth.*

**Table 1.3** Percentage of School Absence out of Maximum Possible Attendance at "Lumley" Lower Secondary School, 1964–1965

|                   | Fall  | Spring |
|-------------------|-------|--------|
| Class 4 (A level) | 2.79  | 6.28   |
| Class 4 (B level) | 5.18  | 7.67   |
| Class 4 (C level) | 7.36  | 12.82  |
| Class 4 (D level) | 16.50 | 16.91  |

*Source*: Hargreaves 1967, 50.

The distinctive characteristics of the two kingdoms can be seen numerically in table 1.3, which shows the absenteeism of the fourth graders rising gradually from A to D. Similar data exist for tardiness, but here the differences are not as significant. More important are Hargreaves's comments. Tardy arrivals are recorded by the student representatives—such as Adrian—who sit by the door and let them in. No one would dare report those from the C and D classes. They would beat you up if you did. But the statements from the students themselves—on whether they would like to stay on for a voluntary fifth year—tell us a lot about their different attitudes to school. Seventy-two percent of the A-level students wish to continue. At all other levels, the number decreases to below 30 percent. Similar differences can be found in school gatherings and social life, which constitute the inner life of the school. A-level students dominate on all occasions, from phys ed to fund-raisers; C- and D-level students are mostly found hanging around on the sidelines.

The students in the fourth-year A-level class, like Adrian himself, were acutely aware of their academic superiority.

Newcomers had a low status in that they held back the rest of the class. Through their shortcomings, these newcomers exposed the class norms. Alf was the most disliked student of the class. He was also the strongest—which the rest of the class accepted—but his strength was in no sense sufficient to compensate for his weaknesses: he was not as capable as the others, did not dress well, and was also more of a trouble-maker. These were all violations of important class norms. Another fundamental rule in the class was, "Do not copy the work of your classmates."

In 4C, this was all turned upside down. The class had three cliques, two of which were respected by the other class-mates, and one of which was looked down on. But here, rank and achievement were inversely related: those with the low-est rank in terms of popularity did the best in school. The punishment for getting good grades was exacting. And in his capacity as their leader, Clint complied with the classroom norms more diligently than anyone else:

> During one math lesson, all the 4C boys were working on vari-ous sections of the textbook. Clint was sitting next to Chris as usual, surrounded by the other clique members. Through-out the lesson, Clint never opened his book or used his pen. He spent the time talking, daydreaming, combing his hair and bullying the younger boys in the class. During study hall periods in the library, he wasted the majority of his time pre-tending to look for a book and playing hide-and-seek with the teacher behind the shelves. All academic activity was avoided scrupulously and flagrantly. Yet judging by the results on the transcripts that he brought with him when he first came to the school, Clint was one of the most intelligent boys at school. And his ingenuity when it came to not getting caught by the teachers when causing trouble was remarkable. Usu-ally he would goad other boys into trouble instead. When a

situation seemed unlikely to provoke any retaliation on the part of the teacher, Clint did not miss out on a single opportunity to break the rules. This approach produced a norm that forbade any kind of academic achievement among his followers.

"… we throw things at each other, cause everyone takes it as a joke and throws things back." … "I like number 79 because he's always messing about. We get a lot of laughs out of him." (Quoted in Hargreaves 1967, 36–37)

Two kings, two kingdoms—but a single territory. And on top of it a system based on emphasizing differences. The A levels were put with the B levels for most activities, and the C levels were put with the D levels. Their schedules were planned accordingly. But the outcome was that of course the students got to know and befriended one another in accordance with this pattern. The gap widened between A and B on the one side, and C and D on the other. The students on "the other side" of the gap seemed more like fairy-tale characters than ordinary children. Other circumstances served to further consolidate this tendency. Most of the appointed class representatives were from the A-level class. The C and D classes compensated for this with physical strength. Excursions and special tasks were reserved for A- and B-level classes. The C and D levels brought little honor to the school, and mainly just caused trouble. They were most useful as subject matter for cautionary tales, serving as examples of the potential abyss that threatened should the students' interest and diligence falter.

*WE MUST ALWAYS BEHAVE LIKE AN A-LEVEL CLASS.* These words were written on a blackboard one day. "Who are you?" a teacher asked a noisy group in the hallway. "We're from 4B, Mr. Teacher." "Well, you sound more like someone from 4E."

These accounts from everyday life at the school are interesting, but of greater importance are the systemically designed dimensions of school differentiation, such as the distribution of experienced teachers. The head teacher and the person who a short time later was appointed head teacher at the neighboring school were, respectively, assigned to the A and B levels—competent educators, impeccable in their discipline, and who consequently always achieved the best results. The teachers assigned to the C and D levels, on the other hand, were second rate and neither could they produce results proving this to be an error in judgment. These teachers employed two different strategies to handle the disciplinary issues of the lower-level classrooms. The first was based on withdrawal. The teacher would sit at their desk, correcting assignments or write reports, while the class was left to live a life of its own. A variation of this strategy entailed simply lecturing at such a volume that any other noise was drowned out, so any deviants in this class might have a chance of learning something. The second was based on domination, or discipline taken to an extreme: any rule violation was countered with harsh punishments. And while it may have seemed as if the students were now doing their work, in reality in this case the students solved the problem with what in Hargreaves's opinion was their own form of withdrawal.

Let me provide an example of how one of the lower-level students is described by a teacher reporting to the head teacher. And let me also cite some of Hargreaves's comments on it. The student is a boy in the D-level class—branded a loser—placed even further down in the hierarchy than the students in C to whom I have paid the most attention so far. Here he is, "Mediocre, improper in every way, lazy, doesn't give two hoots about anyone but himself, vicious, slick, a smoker, uncooperative, paranoid, constantly moaning, a bully, hates anyone who is intelligent, a trouble-maker." And here is Hargreaves's (1967, 100–101) commentary:

> It is hard to imagine a less flattering report. Yet a lot of it was true. Whenever possible, he would shout, scream, and distract other boys. Most of his time at school was spent searching for potential distractions. He would laugh out loud if a teacher told him that his schoolwork would help him get a good job. Most of his actions were directed toward producing a good laugh for himself and his buddies, and he would revel in the guffaws of the rest of the class when he pulled a successful prank and a teacher fell into his trap. When punished, he would sulk if he could not lie his way out of the situation.
>
> Yet this behavior represents an adaptation to the situation. He belongs to an underprivileged class. He has come to learn that he is perceived as a loser. His relationships to the teachers deteriorated steadily over the course of his four years at school, until he was totally rejected by many of them. He made virtually no progress in his schoolwork. … While the A-level class boys advance in ways the teachers find important—and thereby create a learning situation that is rewarding for both teacher and student—the C- and D-level class lads become increasingly slower and more difficult to handle, creating learning situations with little, if any, rewards for either party.

The fundamental traits of a school such as "Lumley" can perhaps be best understood if we view it as a system for twice-over victors—and twice-over losers. Adrian and his minions in the A-level class are victorious first and foremost in relation to the larger scheme of societal demands. The situation in England is as it was among the Sioux people: if one hopes to overcome barriers, schooling is an imperative. Completing school at the highest level possible is the mantra. Passing only primary school is equivalent to no schooling whatsoever. We may attempt to obscure this reality, but will not succeed—neither completely nor for long. Adrian was aware of these circumstances, but so too was Clint. Either the one, long-term prize or nothing at all.

But Adrian emerged victorious, and Clint failed, even in the short term. Parents, teachers, and other adults may be despised or hated, yet countless studies show that somehow their values sneak into the minds and self-perceptions of young people. Be zealous in your studies, read and learn, and obey your masters. Adrian knows this. So does Clint.

On top of all this, the system is there to remind them, have them witness each other's victories and failures, and paint them in light of one another, so the white can become even whiter and the black even blacker. It is a centrifuge in which powerful or powerless individuals, respectively, are condemned to external and extremist positions in an established social order.[7]

In a situation like this, it seems almost self-evident that there is only one remaining option for Clint if he hopes to emerge from all this with his dignity intact. He must believe—and demonstrate that he truly believes—that ordinary adult life is good enough for him and schooling is therefore irrelevant. The best means by which he can uphold this conviction is to begin "living like an adult" as soon as possible, by using the symbols of adulthood. For Clint these symbols are clear enough: smoke and drink, play pool, and chase after girls. And then it's a matter of having control over his own life in all situations other than those involving paid employment, in which the worker slaves away so as to acquire the surplus that will make possible all the adult pastimes mentioned here. So this becomes his response. And the response of his peers. And the response of subsequent C- and D-level classes—as long as we remain within a system that demands such a response in defense of human dignity.

## A PROBABLE FUTURE

Every once in a while someone will ask me what the sociology of schools is. The three studies presented above make this question easy to answer. They all represent, in their own way, sociological studies of schools. Formally speaking they would be categorized as something else. Thabault, who described the village school of Mazières-en-Gâtine, is a former teacher and historian by profession. Wax and his colleagues, who described the Sioux people's school, were anthropologists working with the help of two Sioux natives. Hargreaves, the portrayer of the English school, has an educational background in theology and psychology. Their approaches and methods of study differ as well, ranging from document analysis, interviews, and observations to sociometric tests. Nonetheless, they represent the essence of the sociology. Historical details are welcome to the extent that they can shed light on some of the general conditions of the past. Ethnographic characteristics are only included to shed light on the general belief systems. Teachers as well as students are seen as parts of a whole—and at all times, it is the main attributes and features of this whole that are of key interest. The school is depicted as a system of phenomena, which are connected internally yet always already part of a larger system. If anything, this in particular is the sociology of schools—never mind the definitions.

But this is not, of course, first and foremost the reason why the above-mentioned studies have been chosen and included. They are presented here because each of them, in its own way, tells us something about ourselves. At any rate, it is my hope that the reader has nodded in recognition of at least some of the issues—and felt a bit at home in France, Dakota, and northern England. These nods would indicate above all an appreciation of the general problems at stake in the development of formal schooling. Any society that reaches a certain level of industrial and technological advancement is faced with the need to create formal routines that will attend to the needs of the coming generation. The result is standardized solutions with certain benefits, but also certain costs. National peculiarities surely have a say, but perhaps they have less of a say than we are used to—or comfortable with—ascribing to them.

The flourishing of the village school is first and foremost an example of *the relevant school*. The school had existed in the village long before it was perceived as important. Yet it first became relevant when changes in external factors clearly demonstrated a need for change in the inner structure as well. It became a school in step with the requirements of a given era.

The Sioux people's school came from the outside. It was built on the premise of *the empty rooms*. Learning was forcibly fed. But because the rooms were actually not empty, and because the new knowledge would not help in the life that would later be lived, the strangers' content would never really fall into place and take root.

The third school we called *the centrifuge*—because of the way its inner structure served only to reproduce and reinforce the class divisions of the surrounding society. It is the polarized and polarizing school that produces only more of what the surrounding society already has in abundance.

What the Sioux people's school and centrifuge share—in stark contrast to the village school in Mazières—is that they both became *somebody else's school*. Both studies show the exceeding narrowness of a perspective that solely views the school as a mechanism for bringing up and socializing children, potentially for a society that can—eventually and indirectly—make use of the children's acquired skills. The intention is indoctrination. But once this system, which is called school, has been created, it attains a life of its own— driven by inner and outer forces. It quickly becomes an organism that evolves in accordance with its own internal needs. The school becomes first and foremost—and this is the key to understanding schools such as those in Pine Ridge and Lumley—*the educationists' school*.

And what about us? What about our own schools in relation to the above? If I am right in my supposition that the three studies presented here have some relevance for us, then it probably means that our schools also share—or have shared—some of their characteristics. But here we must proceed with caution and subtlety. It is utterly meaningless to assign grades to our schools, saying, for example, that three parts of Norwegian schools are relevant—one part characterized by the theory of the empty rooms, and two parts by the centrifuge, combined with portions of the educationists' school. Instead we must look at the key elements of this organism, the hows and whats of the school, and perhaps even ask why certain elements are similar while others are completely different. We must endeavor to perceive the school system as a whole. We must also challenge received notions and consider the schools in the context of the greater system—the society to which they belong.

# 2

# SOCIAL ORDER AND THE REACTIONS OF YOUNG PEOPLE

Those who read books, or write them, are used to the fact that language consists of words. They are so used to this fact that they can easily forget that the most important messages perhaps aren't communicated by word of mouth, and definitely not by letters, but rather through body postures, facial expressions or actions, and life conduct. Poets know this and allow their protagonists to speak through actions. Yet social scientists struggle to interpret unspoken and unwritten communication. This, however, should be the primary task of these scientists. They should be trained to read that which isn't expressed in words or—if words are used—lies behind the words. And then they should attempt to communicate through other words, or at least other metaphors, some of what they believe to have understood. The social scientist is an interpreter who tries to help society understand itself. It goes without saying that clear distinctions cannot be made between poetry and sociology.[1]

Let us, with this perspective in mind, consider some of the features that many find typical of young people in industrial societies. I will describe some of these phenomena, attempt to interpret them, and hint at what I believe they tell us about our society. On the basis of this description, we can establish a new foundation for understanding and evaluating the ends served by our schools as well as the young people that the schools encounter.

## AN EPISTLE ON USELESSNESS

It is time to tell a story about a fisherman's wife living somewhere in northern Norway.[2] It will not be a story about hard work and privation, or about a husband who died at sea, and children who ate gruel until the authorities came and gave them split cod instead. No, it will be a story of success. The fisherman was—and is—a good fisherman, and Norway was—and is—a good country. The fisherman fished his way to prosperity and thereby a bigger boat. This meant that he no longer needed to live in a remote location at the mouth of the fjord. It was also advantageous for Norway as a nation that he no longer lived there. It is cheaper and more convenient to have the nation's inhabitants settled in clusters, and therefore the state offered subsidies to those willing to relocate. The fisherman and his family moved into a nice, modern house in a friendly little town.

So far everything was idyllic. And it still is. My point is limited to the observation that the idyll is beginning to show signs of strain. Not once have any of the authorities from children's services ventured into their home, and they probably never will. Yet the fisherman's wife has encountered all the problems that everyone shares, with the only difference being that she sees them more clearly, because for her, they are new.

There was no oil furnace in the house on the fjord. That didn't matter. She had three high-spirited young boys who rushed around the beach and collected driftwood, chopped and stacked it, carried it inside, and built fires in the wood-stoves. The handiest of them filled the lamps with paraffin and poured water from buckets, the strongest fetched water from the well and cleared the pathway to the latrine, and everyone helped to catch fish for the evening stew. And if every chore was completed—and the boys still needed an outlet for their energy—there was always a pile of potatoes to be peeled or nets to be mended.

Then they moved into town. Now water flowed from a tap, heat came from a thermostatically controlled furnace, and the lights had switches. Potatoes were bought in small quantities from the local store; there was no storage space in the small city house. It is unnecessary for me to say more about the predicament of the fisherman's wife. My point should be clear by now. For her, their wonderful children became—as they are now for us—*useless*. Most of their usefulness pertained to chores for a life in a remote location on the seacoast or in comparable settings.[3]

An interesting parallel can be drawn between the relationship of parents and children and the relationship of husband and wife in the modern family. In sociological studies on the family, we commonly claim that the intimate sharing of work between a husband and his wife has become massively reduced. In this situation, the importance of the intimate sharing of emotions has doubled. Romantic love now holds in place the very bonds that were once secured by the common pursuit of holding material privation at bay. Even more extreme, but at the same time less overt, is the situation of many adults in their relationships to children and young people. Our love remains eternal, but it now arises more from the absence of any intimate sharing of work rather than because of it. Married couples are left with only the remnants of a work-related commonality. Instead, spouses are mutual sources of services, pleasure, and long-term guarantees against loneliness. Children and young people are in a similar position, but are becoming increasingly ineffective, useless, an increasingly greater burden, and a source of strain—a fact we are reluctant to acknowledge. Children, youths, persons with disabilities, and unskilled workers have many common characteristics in a modern industrial society such as ours. Everything they can do, others can do better and, above all, more cheaply. We have created a form of society in which it would be for the best if people were born as adults. To redress this, we have made some of them teenagers.

## THE TEENAGER: THE CONTROLLED DEVIANCE

There was a time—not long ago—when the period currently known as adolescence didn't exist to the degree that it does today. From a social perspective—and that is quite important in our case—adolescents were seen as either large children or young women and men. Few people over the age of sixty in Norway have been teenagers. They went from being a child to an adult and were, perhaps, a little bit of both before they made the definitive transition. Most were probably part of a natural community made up of others their age, but they did not—and this is the point—belong to any distinct culture of their own, a specific in-between phase squeezed in between childhood and adulthood. The concept of a "teenager" simply did not exist. There was not as there is now a phenomenon in need of a label, no social category requiring a definition, which would have been further reinforced once the term was coined. The teenage years did not appear out of the blue. They reflect a specific type of society, and a "solution" to a dilemma produced by the currently reigning social order.

What, then, is a teenager? Seen from the outside, it seems easy to answer: a teenager is a person who is between thirteen and nineteen years of age with a somewhat deviant style of dress, is part of a community of others from the same age group, and has insecure, ambivalent, and often conflict-ridden relationships with representatives of other age groups.

If we look just a bit beneath the surface of these truisms, there are three characteristics of teenagers in particular that I find worthy of note here.

First of all, *unproductivity*. Few of us would expect a teenager to contribute anything to the community beyond that of assisting with a few minor chores in the home, and doing a good deed here and there. That's it. Instead, they are supposed to learn with the aim of preparing for a future life and perhaps even an occupation.

The second main characteristic of teenage culture is, as I will call it, an *orientation toward consumption*. This is of course connected to the previous point and is again a reflection of the significance of society's structures. Young people do not enter society as disruptive producers but instead find their most appealing function in the role of consumers.

For the third characteristic of teenage culture, I want to make use of the expression *freedom from responsibility*. This can also be connected to the characteristic of unproductivity. People with no responsibility for production or any other important activity in society will probably have to be allowed a greater margin for deviance in other areas of life. Another word for freedom from responsibility becomes, in this sense, irresponsibility. Objectives become short term; others will take care of the long-term ones. The teenager's life orientation becomes an orientation toward pleasure, which easily becomes a form of consumption. I think that the typical example of freedom from responsibility is found in the Norwegian phenomenon of *russetid*, the period comprising the last half year of upper secondary school for Norwegian students. Here the common norms of public order, alcohol consumption, and sexual conduct are violated in pursuit of a life of somewhat forced, unbridled exuberance. Historically, the tradition probably has its roots in a reaction against tutelage. It is the ritual clashing of a low-status group with its oppressors. But it is—at the same time—a clash that in its form would never be accepted if the protagonists had responsibility for anything other than themselves.

Seen in this light, the teenagers become a direct reflection of the society we live in. We have created a society in which young people are taken out of production. In return, they are encouraged to consume and granted greater leeway when it comes to irresponsible behavior.

Yet in the "solution" described above—echoing our tale of the fisherman's wife—lies also some of the seeds of the downfall of the teenage culture. As you may remember, when the fisherman's wife moved to town, she struggled to find meaningful tasks for her children—while at the same time she was provided with more free time in which to find this problematic. But her problem also became the children's problem. They too experienced their own meaningless uselessness. It

is precisely herein that we find the possibilities for alternative teenage cultures.

## ALTERNATIVE SCENARIOS

Today, a plethora of alternative youth cultures have sprouted
up in contrast to the conventional teenage culture. Most
visible—and the source of greatest horror—are the representatives for the long-haired lifestyle. Most people are aware of
the extreme version here—if only from pictures and terrify-
ing descriptions: long, shaggy manes, beards for those able to
grow them, strange garments, a guitar hung over one shoul-
der, bells around the neck, bare feet in the summertime, and
perhaps insufficient personal hygiene in all seasons. We once
called them hippies, but the hippies died out and became
yippies, and they are supposedly also dead, but the phenomenon isn't dead, and the hair hasn't been cut. It is even possible to sense the effects of it in the most respectable offices
where the length of employees' neck hair has increased by
several centimeters in only a few years. And perhaps it isn't
solely the length of the hair that has changed?

A key aspect of this culture is the choice to be poor. It is
in rich countries that this happens, and among the wealthy
in these countries. In satiety—and with a sidelong glance to
the suffering that afflicts large parts of the world—some people have become anticonsumers. These people have made
deliberate attempts to withdraw from large, impersonal communities and enterprises to cultivate intimate relations with
"whole" human beings instead, as opposed to the thin sliver
of human beings permitted in large organizations. Because
these people are anticonsumers, and because they live in

small communities, they can to a larger extent allow themselves to live in the moment and cultivate an awareness of inner values. Emotions, introspection, and inner experiences are of paramount importance. The question, "What are you?"—implying expectations of a professional specification—is replaced by the question, "Who are you?"—that is, "What kind of human being are you?" which can be said to characterize these ideals. Quantifying such qualities is difficult. The question thereby reinforces an already-pronounced tendency in this culture that values equality and equal status over performance and competition.

The political extremists on the Far Left as well as Far Right are another version of counterculturalists. They are often bitterly opposed to the long-haired specimen, who they believe undermines and depletes the effectiveness of political protest. But what they have in common is the rejection of our type of society. Another commonality is that none of them have the teenage culture's caste-like appearance. Culture is not something they grow into, and then grow out of when they reach the age of twenty. The members may be primarily young, but they could have been old, and some of them are. Membership is a standing that is earned, and its achievement requires great personal courage. Here, counterculture is not marked as being a transitional stage like that of the teenager, whose lifestyle is understood as being something that will be "grown out of." *Russetiden* is once again a useful caricature of the teenage phase: for one period in life, the individual not only can but in fact should flout social conventions and do all the things that neither children nor grown-ups are allowed to do. Because before they know it, adulthood has arrived and all deviance must come to an end. It is the knowledge of this inevitability that makes teenage deviance acceptable for the adult members of the population. On the other hand, due to the uncertainty about whether the counterculturists will in the end resist assimilation into the "normalcy" of socially accepted behaviors and conventions, their lifestyle and attitudes are perceived as a threat.

But our perception of young people could have been altogether different. They could be viewed as trailblazers. They could be seen as people who, precisely because they are young, discern new requirements in the society more rapidly and intensely than others. They could be perceived as people who—often at great personal cost—try out new solutions and forms of community that could perhaps prove valuable for many if society were to take yet another step toward technocracy.

When the technocracy has made further advances, when ordinary people have been deprived of even more activities, when even less air and soil remain, then, finally, it may turn out that it wasn't so stupid that some long-haired and barefoot adolescents or enraged protesters attempted to retrieve the point of balance between need and abundance, between backbreaking toil and the experience of complete uselessness. The counterculturalists can be perceived as trailblazers for all of us. They can be perceived as people who bring along with them something important when they come to school. That is how we will choose to see them here.

## TEENAGE CULTURE AND ITS COUNTERPARTS

The teenage culture is no counterculture. Quite the contrary, it exists in blissful harmony with the main structure

of the industrial society. But the phase beyond teenage culture became a counterculture. The immediate outcome of the
phenomenon known as adolescence is the preservation of
the main structures of society. In the long term, though, the
phenomenon provides the foundation for change by creating
an environment for and attitude of recruitment to a counterculture. Yet what teenagers and counterculturalists have in
common is that they represent key answers for the society
into which they are born. Teenagers and their counterparts
are the product of a technocracy that has no need for them
as young people, but only as adults. If we de-romanticize
our conceptions of youth and acknowledge—not simply
intellectually, but emotionally—its uselessness in a modern
technosociety, then we will at least have arrived at a better
basis for understanding something: teenagers do not come
empty-handed. At the same time, we will have a somewhat
greater possibility of glimpsing some aspects of the school's
responsibilities in relation to young people and society that
are sometimes overlooked.

# 3

## IF SCHOOLS DIDN'T EXIST

Enough has been said about society and youth at this point to allow me to say something about schools. Once again, a few detours are in order. The aim of this chapter is to reveal something about the functions and tasks of schools within the type of society that we have just seen reflected in the reactions of its youngest members. We must not, however, be overzealous in our endeavor to find a solution. A single good question is worth more than a hundred shoddy answers. The underlying question is presented here in the form of a thought experiment.

What would happen to society in its current form if schools didn't exist? If we didn't have a system of teachers, principals, and school administrators, and if most of these weren't situated in large buildings where they met students year-round, year after year, what then—if anything—would be different? And how would society fare?

Not well. At least, it would not fare as it is doing now. But this would perhaps be the case for slightly different reasons than we might normally assume.

## IF SCHOOLS DIDN'T EXIST: ACT I

Schools do close, admittedly. There are breaks, and in Sweden, teachers even go on strike. And we know—parents know, in any case—that the most elementary need satisfied by the school is to provide children with *a place to be*.[1] Cities are not built for children, cars are not built for children, machines do not need them, and adults do not need them. Extended vacations become a burden, and strikes result in catastrophes, simply because our society is not structured to accommodate having children around all the time.

The problem has been turned upside down in the course of one hundred years. In 1871, a commission was established to produce a new education act for Norwegian cities. The commission was unequivocal about the length of the school day: *it should be limited so as not to hinder children from working*. A lengthy quote is in order here, taken from Hans-Jørgen Dokka's (1967, 288–289) seminal work *Fra allmueskole til folkeskole* (From peasant schools to public schools):[2]

> The majority of the commission found it crucial to place substantial import on considerations for the poorest segment of the working population in determining the length of the school day. The commission began by gathering data that would enable a determination of the appropriate amount of compulsory school attendance for working-class children. This was of utmost importance to the commission, for whom the children's school attendance was perceived as an increasingly heavy burden for workers in urban areas—heavier than it had been previously, given the nature of the urban development. The working class that emerged, especially in the larger cities, lived under conditions making them, more or less, dependent on the revenue from their children's labor. Therefore, they should not be forced to comply with compulsory schooling

for any longer than is absolutely necessary. The commission stressed the importance of keeping in mind the fact that children from poor families were sent out to work at a younger age than previously, due to the growing demand for child labor produced by the industrial economy.

The commission's comprehensive findings showed that 26.1 percent of students attending public schools in fifty-six cities—that is, those who had provided the data—worked outside the home in 1871. The percentage-based distribution showed that 15.9 percent maintained "regular employment," while 10.2 percent occasionally carried out "temporary work." The age groups included by the commission were distributed in the following way: 18.3 percent of children were twelve years of age or older, 5.7 percent between ten and years years of age, and 2.1 percent of children were under the age of ten. For seventeen of the cities—among those some of the largest included in the study—more detailed findings specified that 65 percent of children twelve years of age and older were working. This percentage dropped to 34.2 percent for children between ten and twelve years. For the girls, the corresponding figures were 32.7 percent and 15.4 percent, respectively, for the two age groups. There was no information on their incomes, so the commission omitted this data from the study. But the total annual income nonetheless amounted to approximately fifty thousand Norwegian rigsdaler.[3] As would be expected, the oldest students had earned the most, taking home an average of eleven and one-third rigsdaler, compared to seven rigsdaler for the second-oldest group.

The commission did not entertain a single doubt about the importance of the conditions revealed by the data with respect to decisions pertaining to the organization of the schools. Indeed, the commission found it all the more necessary to take child labor into account as it expected—and even hoped—that child labor outside the home would increase beyond the employment rates of 1871. Their data appeared to suggest a clearly inverse proportional relation between child labor and poverty relief.

But the committee's conclusion had little staying power. Educationists protested, and the matter was made the subject of a new study. It was determined that the commission had been exaggerating, and at the very least, the children should not be working that much. As it turned out, the demand for child labor was on the wane. Child mortality rates went down, and the automation of labor continued its unrelenting forward march.

Frank Musgrove (1965) has gathered a large body of data confirming similar conditions in England. A key problem in the earliest phases of industrialization was that children ousted their parents from the workforce. As Musgrove notes, what shocked the bourgeoisie was not the fact that it was children who worked in the mines or factories. Rather, the consternation stemmed from the discovery that they performed better than their parents, who being accustomed to the countryside, had greater difficulties adjusting. Accordingly, the children took home larger salaries, achieving greater freedom and power in the process. In Musgrove's depiction of the past—which is not exactly flattering—laws against child labor were instated in order to protect older people from undue competition. But with the introduction of these laws, coupled with the decline in mortality rates and new technologies, the need for child labor was diminished. In Musgrove's cool words, "Compulsory schools became a necessity in the 1870s, not because children were working, but because to an increasing extent they were not working" (Musgrove 1965, 76).

This does not quite capture the situation in Scandinavia. Our societies were too unified, and our cities were too small. But his words provide a perspective. They do not quite fit with Scandinavia's past, but they can remind us of something in our present—for example, when it was decided that compulsory school attendance should be extended from seven to nine years (act of June 13, 1969, no. 24, effective from July 1, 1971).

Before legislators began addressing the extension of compulsory schooling, four thousand protests arrived through the mail, chiefly from educationists who had experience from the earliest trials on increased school hours. But the Standing Committee on Education and Church Affairs was unwilling to wait. When jobs and social structures are constantly subject to change, the committee argued, this imposes considerable demands on the individual as well as increases the need for a solid general education. This was a recurring theme in the subsequent debate:

> An additional factor in this context that is also of essential significance is the shortage of alternatives for a fourteen- or fifteen-year-old who wishes to leave school. Experience would suggest that this age group has difficulties finding a satisfying job in competition with those who are a little older and, in addition, have completed more years of schooling.
>
> Finally, the committee wants to emphasize that the problems represented by the students suffering the most from "school fatigue" will often be transferred to other parts of society or working life in the event that these students are exempted from compulsory school attendance (Recommendation to the Odelsting XLV, 1968–1969, 5).

It was self-evident for the committee that schools should assume responsibility for these young people. This assumption was also self-evident for the majority of those who would later discuss the question in Parliament. Einar Hovdhaugen provides an example (Odelstinget debate, April 21, 1969, 273):[4]

When one is confronted with these problems (people who are "tired of school" and have disciplinary problems), it is natural that the question arises as to whether the last years of lower secondary school should be voluntary. It would be the simplest and least demanding solution for our schools. It would probably have been easier to approve this solution about twenty to twenty-five years ago than it is today due to the structure of our society. Today the opportunities through which a fourteen- or fifteen-year-old can enter the workforce and receive training are limited. In most cases, these opportunities are nonexistent. Economic development has left the fourteen- or fifteen-year-old children of today with little motivation for working regular hours. Today, an increasing number of people reside in cities and densely populated areas. What is more, with the family waning in its power and influence, there is cause to fear that students who leave school when they are fourteen or fifteen years old will in many cases face unemployment and join juvenile gangs, and on the whole mature in such a way as to create greater problems for society than the problem the school faces in terms of the issue of nine years of compulsory school attendance. Therefore, nine years of compulsory schooling is favorable under the assumption that our schools will be better equipped to accommodate today's challenges than they are at present. Should we abandon the scheme of compulsory education for nine years, I fear that (schools would) … fail to meet their social and pedagogical responsibilities.

There wasn't any real debate about increasing the general school attendance from seven to nine compulsory years. Within the Norwegian Parliament, Bjarne Undheim was the strongest skeptic, but he found it unrealistic to propose any initiatives against compulsory schooling.[5] Teddy Dyring, another member of Parliament, drafted a proposal that compulsory schooling should last only until eighth grade.[6] His point of view was rather unusual (Lagtinget debate, 1969, 59): "For those who are 'tired of school,' those who are not motivated to continue their education, the school is no school, but rather a form of housing."

The proposal received four votes and was virtually ignored in the debate. The matter was already as good as resolved. But there was a minor deliberation about whether some individuals, in extraordinary cases, should be allowed to leave school after eight years.

The majority of the members of the Standing Committee on Education and Church Affairs favored the wording proposed by the department: "A student may, in special cases, be discharged earlier, but not before he has received eight years of schooling." The current law takes a similar approach. But a small minority considered a proposal that was originally suggested by the Norwegian Teachers' Union: "The school board may under special circumstances decide to transfer a student from ordinary class instruction into an alternative learning facility." Many fought enthusiastically for this clause. The minority group's captain, Torger Hovi, stated that (Odelstinget debate, April 21, 1969, 264)[7]

> I find it difficult to make sense of the conclusion drawn by the majority on this matter. When a student is discharged, the school has lost its grip on the student—along with its responsibility. And yet the student remains society's responsibility. On the other hand, our society does not have any other institutions with better resources than the school to deal with such matters. Therefore, the minority does not want to grant anyone the right to discharge a student before completion of nine years of schooling. ...
>
> [W]hen a student is discharged, the school has lost its grip on him.

This is actually something we all know, and yet it often remains unarticulated. This, in turn, is never a good pedagogical starting point: "Come on, go to school, we have no better solution." In such cases, it is probably better to think of society as the great benefactor, sacrificing everything to ensure that the little ones are offered some small part of our cultural heritage.

This is probably also true. But it is not the whole and absolute truth. There are also other reasons why we have schools. If we are to understand the school, we must attempt to shed light on these other reasons. And if these reasons are found acceptable, we must try to organize the school accordingly. If they are deemed unacceptable, we must try to prevent the needs behind such reasons from arising in the first place—or address them in another manner.

From this perspective it thus *also* becomes important to view the school as a storage facility—a particularly expedient means of removing children and youths from general circulation in society. We have no idea what to do with children, young people, and others rendered deviant by the requirements of working life. We have one or maybe two ideas: retire them or place them in an institution. What is meant by "institution" is first and foremost "school"—that is, the ordinary schools designed for children and young people from the age of seven to fifteen. In terms of numbers, we are able to keep no small number of "useless" individuals out of circulation through schools. We have created a technically sophisticated, industrialized, and mass-producing society in which young people are just as useless as most other forms of unskilled labor. The issue of teenagers and their counterculture is intimately bound up with their uselessness, depending on what society defines as important. In this case, the school is a particularly expedient medium for containment.

Through schools, the encounter between the society of the useless and that of the adults is postponed. If schools didn't exist, we would have to devise another strategy, and more important, find another purpose for young people.

## IF SCHOOLS DIDN'T EXIST: ACT II

Another important aspect of our societies would also lose its potency if schools were to close. It is an aspect seldom mentioned around the dinner tables of the wealthy, but frequently addressed over dinner among ordinary folks. It is an obvious fact for most parents—and will soon be for most children—that certain types of schooling are highly decisive for one's future. Table 3.1 provides a succinct impression of the high—and increasingly higher—level of awareness of this reality on the part of both parents and children. For the uninitiated: in some school subjects, it is possible for the students themselves to decide the level of difficulty at which they want to work. Tier one is the easiest, and tier three is the hardest, so nobody needs to feel bad about not measuring up.

But ultimately, many people are nonetheless disappointed; they bite off more than they can chew. Because they know, as their parents know, and as most people know, that a certificate for having passed lower secondary school in the lowest tier isn't even worth the price of the paper it is printed on. During the second half of the school year, schools are granted the authority to force students into the tier where they "belong." My guess is that schools are reluctant to exercise this authority. They too know what the rest of us know. Here, something else is at work that extends beyond the

**Table 3.1** Three-Tier Distribution in Percent of Eighth-Grade Students by School Subject, between 1964–1965 and 1968–1969

Tier distribution in subjects

| Year | Norwegian | | | Math | | | English | | | German | | Not German |
|---|---|---|---|---|---|---|---|---|---|---|---|---|
| | 1 | 2 | 3 | 1 | 2 | 3 | 1 | 2 | 3 | 1 | 2 | |
| 1964–1965 | 1.5 | 31.6 | 54.8 | 15.2 | 29.6 | 51.8 | 13.3 | 27.9 | 51.6 | 13.4 | 51.8 | 34.8 |
| 1965–1966 | 9.7 | 30.5 | 56.9 | 14.4 | 29.2 | 53.0 | 14.0 | 27.0 | 53.9 | 15.1 | 54.1 | 30.8 |
| 1966–1967 | 9.7 | 30.7 | 56.1 | 14.3 | 29.3 | 51.7 | 13.1 | 27.2 | 54.2 | 16.0 | 53.4 | 29.0 |
| 1967–1968 | 9.0 | 29.2 | 59.1 | 13.5 | 29.5 | 54.1 | 13.3 | 26.8 | 56.0 | 15.5 | 54.1 | 29.1 |
| 1968–1969 | 8.0 | 27.3 | 61.3 | 12.2 | 27.3 | 57.6 | 12.2 | 25.5 | 59.4 | 14.9 | 57.0 | 27.7 |

*Source:* National Curriculum Committee, Recommendation I, Oslo, 1970, 45, 49.

platitudes of the public school's declared objectives. Here, it is a matter of granting admission passes to the class structure of society. Here, it is neither a question of learning or living. It is a question of being able to demonstrate some form of justification when moving forward in the race. The table illustrates clearly that most students have learned something in the course of their time in school. The third-tier enrollment rates are increasing steadily.

This shift has been observed and noted by many—for example, by Tore Lindbekk (1971, 19–20):[8]

> On the whole, the attitude of the surrounding society has been that an increase in schooling will increase the actual competence of students in school—i.e., the students' utility value. The amount of this increase in utility value remains an open question. In the meantime, school attendance records and the schools' grading system have been implemented as important conflict-reducing criteria for the selection process involved in the allocation of attractive positions within society. Few recruiting institutions attach much importance to these criteria as actual indicators of real utility. There is assumed to be a positive correlation between level of education, grades, and relevant occupational proficiency. But no industries or organizations have ever gone to the trouble of investigating the problem in further depth. What they care about is that these criteria are fair. And discounting these criteria would just generate complaints and extra work.
>
> In this regard, it is probably through its classification of individuals as bearers of rights that the school system today makes its most needed and evident contribution to other institutions.

An unstoppable growth factor is built into this logic, the impact of which is illustrated in figure 3.1. Where the most important privileges in society are underpinned by the educational structure, the fight for these special advantages

Number of students

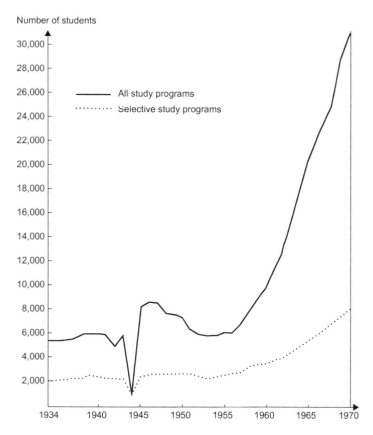

**Figure 3.1** Total number of students attending Norwegian institutions of higher learning between 1934 and 1970. *Source:* Norwegian Research Council for Science and the Humanities (NAVF).

will unfold at increasingly higher levels. There was a time when primary and lower secondary school attendance functioned reasonably well as an access point to advantages for the minority. With nine years of compulsory schooling, this access point has literally been brought down to earth. Everyone begins here, so the first stage of development must be those stages that come *in addition*. But lo and behold, that creates inequality! Almost like a law of nature, we will soon hear the calls for twelve years of compulsory schooling, so once again everyone will be placed on an equal footing. Yet again a stratification layer is removed: everyone begins on equal terms starting in the thirteenth year, and the fight for the scarce goods continues. And it will probably proceed in this way until some day the bubble bursts—and there will be no workers on hand to do the small number of jobs that are left to be done.

If schools didn't exist, society would still need a way to funnel its citizens into the various jobs found in society. And if schools didn't exist, it seems likely that society would *initially* fall back on that which, still today, determines the level of educational achievement needed by the student in order to make do: the social position of the family.

Study after study comes to exactly the same conclusion: there is a crucial correlation between the family's social position (measured as the parents' professional standing) and the child's completed level of schooling. The level of schooling, in turn, becomes a crucial factor in terms of the social position of the child. This circle is so tightly knit—and with so few exceptions—that it would be tempting to suggest that we would be better off without it altogether. At least, then, it would be impossible to ignore the actual connection between heredity and status. It would no longer be hidden behind a purportedly transparent system.

In his dystopian novel from 1966, Michael Young warns against intelligence as a mechanism for class distinction, or as stated in the original title, *The Rise of the Meritocracy, 1870–2033: An Essay on Education and Equality*.[9] This is like warning against flooding in the Sahara! By shouting so loudly about the dangers of a society that is controlled by intelligent subjects extracted from the school system, Young does nothing more than divert attention away from the reality. If anything, the educational system just confirms the social differences that already exist. It provides people of high status with *special* opportunities for taking exams. Their status within the class structure of society thus becomes the most robust form of status—awarded by birth and achieved by schooling. The myth of Young—corroborated by the celebrated examples of *extraordinary individuals* who have managed to break through the limitations of their heritage and educate themselves into the upper echelons of society—only contributes to obscuring the fact that *most people* stay where they are born. Should advancement occur, it occurs for the class in its entirety. And in the meantime, the class above has also advanced.

Table 3.2 offers a glimpse of the typical research findings in this field. These figures are from England, but similar findings can be procured from closer or more distant locations.[10] The table shows the failure rates at an English upper secondary school. The worst-performing students have already been eliminated. Nonetheless, the majority are still doing poorly, compared to the children from upper-class homes. Here only 10 percent of the upper third have failed versus 54 percent in the "unskilled worker" category—assessed at the time of

**Table 3.2**   Failure Rates at an English High School, in Relation to the Father's Employment Status and Student's Results on Admission

|                                       | Result on admission |              |             |
|---------------------------------------|---------------------|--------------|-------------|
| Father's occupational category        | Upper third         | Middle third | Lower third |
| Business and trade                    | 10                  | 25           | 34          |
| Office administration                 | 19                  | 32           | 42          |
| High-skilled work                     | 38                  | 58           | 62          |
| Low-skilled work                      | 54                  | 62           | 76          |

*Source*: Boalt and Husén 1964, 79.

admission. Among the lower third, 34 percent from the highest social class versus a total of 76 percent of the children of unskilled workers have failed. What the numbers represent here is presumably the effects of numerous minor centrifuges of the type illustrated through the examples of Adrian and Clint in chapter 1.

This pattern continues from the lowest to the highest levels of school. We *know* it is like this. Reaching the top of the educational ladder—legitimately achieving the admission passes that some students were born to obtain—is an achievement predominantly reserved for children from wealthy backgrounds. And should they fail to achieve and receive their admission passes through the ordinary channels at home, they can easily obtain them through a detour to some foreign university.[11] If the schools ceased to exist, a veil would be torn away.[12] We would experience firsthand the significance of birthright. And we would be obliged to discuss in a serious manner who, if anyone, should receive most of society's spoils—in rank or wealth—and on what grounds.

## IF SCHOOLS DIDN'T EXIST: ACT III

For some, one implication is as clear as the blue sky: the transfer of skills would be lost if schools didn't exist. A modern-day, increasingly complicated society calls for increasingly more schooling of its young members. The cultural heritage is growing, and that necessarily requires the allocation of more time for the transfer of knowledge. Our intellectual development and the foundation of our material welfare rest on this legacy.

If countries with different levels of education are compared, there is an almost-perfect correlation between a country's gross domestic product and average levels of education. Developing nations invest in education for a good reason. Without school, no development. The school is the bedrock on which everything rests. This much was clear in the example of the French village presented in the first chapter of this book.

Nevertheless, it may still be entirely wrong.

*For a while* the French village school became the bedrock on which everything rested. Something similar was probably also the case in Norway. What Thabault shows in depth and detail to be true for the small French village, Dokka demonstrates to be true for the entire Norwegian school system. There was *a genuine need* for schools. They were the underlying condition for continued material growth. They disseminated letters, numbers, and techniques. They made new political forms possible and became caretakers of the cultural heritage.

For a period of time, they did all this so thoroughly that the school became a given for most of us. But our time is different from Thabault's. Our time is not what Dokka describes. Our time must become ours.

Correlations are not causes. The apparent connection between levels of education and economic growth can also reflect the various functions I have mentioned above—storage and social stratification—which increase in accordance with the gross domestic product.[13]

As the size of our cultural heritage increases, so too do our archives. Here we arrive at a key point. The French village school was—as were our original public schools—established in a phase *between* the subsistence economy and the arrival of a fast-paced, technocratic society. As Musgrove (1965, 26) writes, "If a generation in a primitive society forgets to do its homework, its culture will be lost." In *our* time, on the other hand, we are free to look up whatever information we need; it exists somewhere, accessible to anyone who takes the trouble to learn the most basic techniques of looking things up or digging things out. But in those interim years, only schools provided this possibility. As the culture burgeoned and expanded, the bubble of knowledge eventually burst—and soon enough, water pumps, mealtimes, and apprenticeships were no longer sufficient to transfer the ever-increasing volumes of knowledge. Schools solved all these problems—for the time being at least.

The volume of knowledge has subsequently grown at a rate almost impossible to fathom. Figure 3.2 provides an overview of the access to technical and scientific literature in the University Library[14] and twelve other faculty and scientific libraries in Denmark. The vertical scale is logarithmic, meaning that the relative distance between values on the scale decreases as the scale ascends, so the increase is far

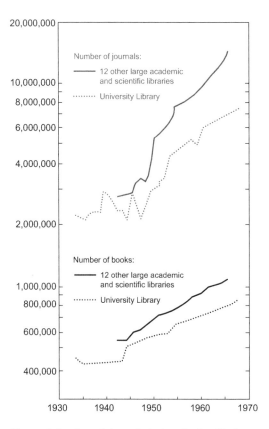

**Figure 3.2** Growth in technical and scientific literature at the University Library and twelve other academic and scientific libraries in Denmark, 1933–1969. Logarithmic scale. *Source:* Ruby 1970.

more dramatic than it might at first appear to the untrained eye. The number of books has doubled within the University Library over the course of thirty years and within the other libraries over the course of twenty. The number of journals has doubled over the course of fourteen and nine years, respectively, while the number of articles within the journals has increased by over 50 percent in the last decade.[15] Even if the school increased the volume of its curriculum every year, it would inevitably fail: the snippet of knowledge covered in schools will become smaller and smaller in relation to the total volume of all there is to know. We will never again be able to dream about a *knowledgeable* citizenry. Our ultimate goal must instead be to provide that citizenry with the tools and curiosity to look.

And still we cling to a form of schooling based on the model of the village school. But the village was a closed society. This also meant that its inhabitants *knew their* society: they had an overview; they lived within a microcosm. When this bubble burst and society was flooded with new information, the need for new forms of communication arose. Only then did a school arrive. Yet *our* society is open to the point of despair. We have knowledge about everything—in books, in archives, and on tape. What *we* need is overview, an entirety, to seal up the bubble anew. We need a system that re-creates the village situation before the school arrived.[16]

Our situation is thus new in several ways. We are living in a phase in which the knowledge of each discipline is increasing at such a remarkable rate that the schools manage to grapple with only a fraction of all that knowledge every year. This is especially true within the fields of mathematics, chemistry, physics, and biology, but it also holds true for the humanities and social sciences. We cannot possibly retain everything there is to know about these subjects. The best we can do is learn the general principles and techniques for finding knowledge. At the same time, though, as our knowledge—viewed in comparison to the current ongoing expansion of information and knowledge—is increasingly less, we are becoming *more and more ignorant of our own society*. We are becoming more ignorant in both absolute and relative terms. Few are able to maintain an overview of the continuous stream of social science publications because it is so dense, so swift, and so difficult. Both here and in other disciplines, it has become impossible to communicate anything more than an ever-diminishing fraction of this information and knowledge to schoolchildren. In addition, it is unlikely that the increase in the number of books and articles will manage to keep up with the increase in complexity and lack of transparency in our society. Everyone says that social science research continues to provide us with greater knowledge about our societies. This appears to be true in the sense that the sheer volume of books and articles is ever increasing. But it seems questionable if we consider the formal increase of knowledge in terms of this growing complexity and insuperability. Nobody has measured or quantified this, but as a means of highlighting my main point, I want to claim that ignorance about social life actually increases faster than the amount of knowledge contained in books. In spite of the incredible development of social science research— seen within all industrialized societies—I would thus argue that the residents of the French village actually knew a lot more about their society than almost anybody knows about ours. Even if social science were the only subject in school, it would be to no avail.

We are living in a different era. We must rethink and explore the potential for other ways by which schools could contribute to reestablishing a sense of unity and transparency in society. We must discover alternative ways of learning how to live in society.

# 4

## POWER IN SCHOOLS

Many things would change if schools didn't exist. This is probably the main reason why they aren't discontinued, why they continue to function as they have always done, and why we keep getting more of the same. But there are many other reasons for why the school endures. A school is like an organism that continues to grow all on its own and will keep doing so until some of the elements of its internal constitution are transformed. In this chapter, I will discuss the conditions required to bring about this internal transformation.

### "A PART OF LIFE"

Many people feel that schools have multiple purposes. Some individuals have taken note of this and at least made an effort to adapt the school to these myriad purposes. The Norwegian Parliament has also felt and observed this, and attempted its own adaptive measures. As I will illustrate below, however, the latter efforts are bound to fail. But let us first take a look at the aspirations of the Norwegian Parliament, as found in the preamble of the revised Act concerning Primary and Lower Secondary Education (June 13, 1969, no. 24):

> The primary and lower secondary school shall, in agreement and cooperation with the families, contribute to providing all students with a Christian and moral upbringing, foster the development of their abilities, both those of mind and body, and provide them with a solid general education, so as to enable them to become useful and independent human beings at home and in society.
>
> The school shall promote freedom of spirit and tolerance, and endeavor to facilitate constructive modes of cooperation between teachers and students, and between schools and families.

There has been no small amount of struggle over each and every word in these paragraphs. Politicians and educators, administrators and parents, have all spent time in the trenches. But considerable doubt remains concerning the meaning of the term "useful human beings," and even greater doubt as to how they are to be created. Some things are clear, though. The students are to receive a Christian upbringing, a good, general education, and develop their abilities. Beyond this, mention is made of something that was not included in the previous version of the act and therefore is of special importance: the students must now become "useful and *independent*." The act of 1959 did not go any further than "useful." And now they must become so both at home *and* in society. Previously, emphasis was placed only on society. Finally, and most important, the entire final paragraph of the preamble is new. It was not proposed by the committee writing the new act. Nor did it come from the ministry. Yet the Norwegian Parliament deemed it essential to include freedom of spirit, tolerance, and constructive modes of cooperation. The Standing Committee on Education and Church Affairs argued that

> it is just as important for the individual to realize his or her skills and interests as it is to foster good attitudes in the students. To this end, the school environment plays a pivotal role. We must therefore, to a much greater extent, begin to view our schools as social communities. Schools can and must do more than prepare and qualify students for the life ahead of them. Schools are in their own right an essential part of life. Education has become—and will be even more so—an increasingly integral part of what it means to be a human being. Schools must therefore have an intrinsic value. Children and young people should be able to find joy in their existence while attending school. It will hence become a key responsibility for schools to promote well-being and happiness. (Recommendation to the Odelsting XIV, 1968–1969, 9)

If storage was indeed inevitable, it could hardly take place under better conditions than those outlined by the Standing Committee on Education and Church Affairs.

When things didn't turn out as intended—and will not despite the new amendments—it is first and foremost because the Norwegian Parliament left the schools in the hands of the educationists. That sounds like a vile thing to say—and this is exactly how it is intended. I am, naturally, not referring to those who populate our schools. When I say "educationists," I am referring to the experts and public servants. This "vile" sentiment was expressed perhaps most plainly in a speech given by Tønnes Andenæs, rephrasing an old saying before the Norwegian Parliament: the field of medicine is too important to be left in the hands of doctors.[1] Something similar could be said about our universities. They are too important for the development of our society to be left to their own devices, in the same way as industrial matters are too important for significant parts of our society to be left in the hands of the people running those industries. And yet we do this all the time, producing nothing but unequal growth and hidden expenditures. But I digress. The subject at hand is the schools.

The underlying cause of many of the current challenges—some of which I will discuss below—stems from contradictions embedded in the Norwegian Parliament's ambitions. Not only do they aspire to create a healthy living space, but *also* an efficient space for learning the traditional skills for which schools were initially designed. And so they entrust both the nurturing of life and efficient teaching to staff who, until now, have only specialized in the latter. In the following, much of my critique will be directed toward the existing forms of education and current state of its personnel. But we are equally at fault. Without providing any clear instructions, we have asked specialists to do one thing, while in addition to this and sometimes even in opposition to it, have expected them to do something else entirely.

## A FRAMEWORK FOR EDUCATIONISTS

The new amendment to the Act concerning Primary and Lower Secondary Education is, above all, a *framework*. It specifies a few learning objectives and some basic guidelines. But decisions about its contents were left to others. At some point, two general options existed in terms of who these "others" could be: either low-level politicians, such as municipal politicians, or even parental representatives, on the one hand, or public servants, on the other, ranging from the secretary of education down to the youngest teacher in the classroom. Responsibility fell on the latter. Yet this was not the original intention. We will explore this matter in further detail below. For now, it is sufficient to establish who is given responsibility for the contents of the framework. The ministry is mentioned seventy-four times in the Act concerning Primary and Lower Secondary Education. We will look closely at two of these cases.

## A NATIONAL CURRICULUM

The most recent Primary and Lower Secondary Education Act (Section 7) states that

> the Ministry will determine, after having heard expert opinions on its contents, the Curriculum Guidelines for Compulsory Education, which will serve to specify the objectives that have been set for schools, including lesson plans, schedules, and subject-specific blueprints for all standard, supplementary, and special classes.
>
> The lesson plans in the Curriculum Guidelines are to be compulsory for all schools, with the exception of schools offering additional instruction beyond the minimum number of school hours as determined by Parliament in Section 6. For the lower grades, however, up to six hours of the minimum requirement can be devoted to specific subject areas pending approval by the board of education.

The committee of experts was appointed in 1967 under the self-chosen name of the National Curriculum Committee (*Normalplanutvalget*). It consisted exclusively of educationists. At one large-scale committee meeting, only one out of fifty-one participants did not hold a position at a school or university. This person was the secretary. The committee chair, Dokka, was a former teacher and associate professor in educational science at the time. Their activities resulted in two reports: "Preliminary Study for a National Curriculum for Compulsory Education" (referred to here as the National Curriculum Committee, 1970, Recommendation I), and "Proposal for National Curriculum for Compulsory Education" (referred to here as National Curriculum Committee, 1970, Recommendation II). The former provides us with a series of fundamental considerations as well as the history behind the curriculum, and the latter with a list of the specific materials suggested for all public schools in Norway. In the "An Open Curriculum" section in chapter 5 of this book, I will take a closer look at the Ministry of Education's interpretation of these reports as this found expression in the Curriculum Guidelines for Compulsory Education (*Mønsterplan for grunnskolen* 1971).

No national curriculum existed when the first public schools were created. Well, actually something similar did exist. Bishop Pontoppidan (1698–1764) was responsible for the interpretations of the scriptures at the time, and pastors, senior rectors, and other bishops took care of the remaining guidelines. As biblical texts waned in importance, a long period of independence followed—until the administration gradually began to grow. Municipal education commissioners soon arrived, making recommendations for their school districts. The recommendations were copied and centralized, leading to the first version of a national curriculum stipulating educational requirements for all public schools throughout the country in 1939. The contents presented there were formulated as *minimum requirements for the schools*; the curriculum was intended to apply to all students. The minimum requirements were to be understood as an average. Some students would not fulfill all of them, while others would fare better.

With this in mind, the National Curriculum Committee (1970, Recommendation I, 103) attempted to accommodate these variations by ascribing greater degrees of freedom to each school:

> The new national curriculum is not intended to serve as a simple formula for how and what to teach in each subject in school. It should be viewed as a guiding framework: as previously noted, the Primary and Lower Secondary Education Act underscores the importance of local influence—whereby the school boards, individual schools, and individual teachers will have greater influence on the shaping of the school and its contents. In correlation with this, the national curriculum will offer a series of suggestions while at the same time invite local stakeholders to have the final say in deciding the contents. These measures are, furthermore, necessary in the interest of providing for the potentially large variations in the number of classes and lessons assigned in the lower grades. It is, in this regard, of central importance to emphasize that the contents proposed by the national curriculum should not be considered compulsory for everyone. The scope pertains above all to the potential and likely additions to the number of lessons in the different subjects that might be expected to occur.

It sounds like unbridled freedom will reign in the Norwegian school system. This was hardly the intention. The deeds of the National Curriculum Committee countervail its promises. The committee's position on grading provides an illustrative case in point. Not only do the committee members accept the traditional notion of grading, but they encourage an increased centralization of the grading scheme throughout the public school system. As Recommendation I (201) states,

> During performance assessments in primary and lower secondary schools, the student must always be evaluated in relation to classmates from the same year. The student's performance is thus not to be assessed on the basis of absolute standards, or on the basis of more or less clearly defined notions of quality or performance ratings. Performance viewed in relation to a larger and representative group will serve as the foundation for ranking the level of the student or the entire class.

Their position on grading is hit home in Recommendation II (76):

> As students advance through primary and lower secondary school, the necessity for an evaluation of the actual progress of the student's personal and academic development increases. Such awareness of the student's progress will be a matter of growing interest for the students, their parents, and the school. Ascertaining the actual abilities and progress of each student is especially important as the student transitions from school to work or higher education.
>
> On assessing the progress of each student, it is not the individual student's performance that is to be evaluated but rather the performance of a group of students viewed as a whole in relation to defined standards or stipulated norms. Each student's progress will then be assessed in relation to his or her peers in such a way that his or her performance level is determined in relation to his or her year. These measures are based on the notion of primary and lower secondary schools as public schools, and as such, definitive requirements held to be valid for all students cannot be imposed.

The seemingly unquestionable benefits of being compared to a large group of peers—the actual important reference group—instead of in relation to the learning targets put forth by the National Curriculum Committee—are not immediately evident. Regardless, the intention is clear: all students are to be assessed by the same standards. Whether or not the national curriculum is to be viewed as a *minimum requirement*, average requirement, or guideline is a matter of complete indifference insofar as the authors simultaneously insist on enforcing a rigorous control system to carefully rank students, teachers, and schools according to the students' success in learning the curriculum. Behold the brave student who, near the completion of seventh grade, stands up and says, "I refuse to go along with this! It runs counter to the Standing Committee on Education and Church Affairs' promise that I should find joy in my existence while attending school." It would take an even braver teacher to listen.[2]

*And in what way, then, must the students outperform their peers?*

The Primary and Lower Secondary Education Act intimates an answer to this question. Section 7 lists the most important school subjects: "The school curriculum must cover Christianity, Norwegian, math, foreign languages, physical education, local geography, social studies, [and] natural sciences as well as studies in aesthetic, practical, and social matters." As for the instruction of Christianity studies, the requirements are specified in the act: all students "must become familiar with the main topics of the Bible, the central developments of the church, and the Christian teachings according to the Evangelical-Lutheran creed." The act continues, "In coordination with the instruction in social studies, Christianity studies must provide an overview of other religions and views of life, including the general aspirations towards peace and harmony between nations."

The rest is left to the discretion of the National Curriculum Committee. Table 4.1 illustrates the subjects to be included and the designated hours for each as suggested by the committee. There are few hints in the committee's recommendations as to why exactly these subjects and the number of hours for each subject are recommended. Most probably, and also most understandably, the designated hours for each subject are the product of compromises between competing school subjects.[3] Or as Dokka (1971, 62) candidly states, "During our work, we have also relied, to some extent at least, on our common knowledge of how the school actually is and an assessment of how it will be able to develop. It would indeed be close to impossible to form a lesson plan without pedagogical knowledge and estimates based on practical experiences."

The wording of another statement is a bit harsher: school subjects are chosen because they have been chosen before, and because we have teachers educated in these subjects to serve as instructors. Mathematics is a useful example. Math skills are undeniably essential for both well-being and lunar explorations, but are they relevant for the ordinary lower secondary school student? Yet throughout all lower secondary schools, the National Curriculum Committee has determined that students will spend four hours a week on this subject. Only the study of Norwegian requires an equal number of hours. There is not even a footnote mentioning the possibility that we might be better off without this requirement. Anyone wishing to learn how to take apart an engine can learn to do so by taking an elective. But to demand that everyone learn what only a tenth of the class will ever use makes it hard to see such arrangements as anything but a

**Table 4.1** Distribution of Hours for All Subjects in Primary and Lower Secondary School, Based on the National Curriculum Committee's Recommendations, 1971

| | Grades | | | | | | | | | |
|---|---|---|---|---|---|---|---|---|---|---|
| | 1 | 2 | 3 | 4 | 5 | 6 | 7 | 8 | 9 | Total |
| Christianity | 2 | 2 | 2 | 2 | 2 | 1 | 2 | 1 | 2 | 16 |
| Norwegian including handwriting | 5 | 5 | 5 | 4 | 5 | 5 | 4 | 4 | 4 | 41 |
| Mathematics | 3 | 3 | 4 | 4 | 3 | 4 | 4 | 4 | 4 | 33 |
| English | | | | 2 | 2 | 3 | 3 | 3 | 3 | 16 |
| Local geography | 2 | 2 | 2 | | | | | | | 6 |
| Social science | | | | 2 | 2 | 4 | 3 | 4 | 4 | 19 |
| Natural sciences | | | | 2 | 2 | 3 | 4 | 4 | 3 | 18 |
| Music | 1 | 1 | 1 | 2 | 2 | 1 | 2 | | | 10 |
| Arts and crafts | 1 | 1 | 2 | 4 | 4 | 4 | 3 | 2 | | 21 |
| Physical education | 1 | 1 | 2 | 2 | 2 | 2 | 2 | 2 | 2 | 16 |
| Home economics | | | | | | | 3 | | | 3 |
| Electives | | | | | | | | 6 | 8 | 14 |
| Total | 15 | 15 | 18 | 24 | 24 | 27 | 30 | 30 | 30 | 213 |

doltish residue from a struggle that was, at some point in time, initiated to combat widespread innumeracy. Where is the analysis of the actual needs of our children today? Under what rock must we search to find an example of the important research conducted on the life awaiting students on leaving school, or the analyses of what representatives from other levels of the education system have to say about the skills and abilities developed in primary and lower secondary schools? It is not hard to imagine that the advocates of a system intent on conveying a narrow agenda of filling jobs and social positions would grow anxious when listening to such analyses. Yet such an agenda must eventually confront the systematic research telling us that the exact opposite is needed. It is not knowledge acquisition but instead the ability to seek out knowledge that is required today. It is not about attaining information or fragments of reality but rather the ability to work with these pieces of reality over an extended period of time, articulating problems and discerning totalities. A different recommendation from the School Committee of 1965 (41–42), also referred to as the Steen Committee, published in the same year as the appointment of the National Curriculum Committee makes reference to some of these general skills, including specific suggestions for content:[4]

> Of primary importance for the majority of the participants in the survey was the demand for general, study-related skills. Specifically, these skills involved the ability to identify the main points of a text, note taking, advanced literacy, and the ability to scrutinize, compare, and discuss data—in short, the ability to collect information in a library, and apply this information in an essay or reports of various kinds.

A similar line of reasoning is found in a recommendation for upper secondary schools. Nevertheless, our primary and lower secondary schools have become subject-based schools. This much is clear in reading the National Curriculum Committee's recommendation. It is not until the section in which the purpose and contents of *each subject* in school is listed that we find even the slightest mention of what is clearly the most fundamental question:

*WHY IS OUR CURRICULUM CURRICULUM?*

The aspirations of the Primary and Lower Secondary Education Act are becoming increasingly blurred here. Each subject, Recommendation I (108) states, hereunder their "logic and structure, types of problems and assignments, and compatibility with other subjects, must be respected." A little further down on the same page the point is driven home with even greater clarity: it should be the school *subjects*, not the Parliament, that determine the learning requirements.

> If the total amount of subject matter to be covered by the schools is to remain within reasonable boundaries, this will entail letting go of the idea that each subject will "cover everything." It is, however, critical that these curtailments be based on specific principles to prevent elimination of the essential materials from the subject in question. For some subjects, it will make sense to prioritize the most *elementary* or fundamental aspects of the subject, while for other subjects there will be an emphasis on more *typical* or *general* aspects. *In general, it should be endeavored to include subject matter that based on a professional assessment, is of the greatest value and interest.*

The use of italics in the last sentence was my own doing. I did so because the sentence answers our question. The quote says little about why certain subjects are chosen in the first place, but instead tells us why our schools have become structured around the subjects, once these have been chosen. A product of manifold interests and compromises, each subject sluggishly makes its way into the curriculum. *Once there*, the specialists are called in to decide which elements are of the most value and interest.

This final process is the central focus of the National Curriculum Committee's Recommendation II. Throughout more than four hundred pages, discussing in detail the subject matter deemed most worthwhile for the public school curriculum—from Christianity studies to public support services—the document scrutinizes everything from the contents and methods to the recommended subject-specific requirements for students on completing school.

The words of the lawmakers drift off into the distance— "an essential part of life," a place with "an intrinsic value," a place where children and youths "find joy in their existence," and "a key responsibility for schools to promote well-being and happiness"—and the phrases all fade away, for there are no *people* assigned to prioritize these ends in what is falsely labeled the school community. Look again at the division of subjects and hours presented above (table 4.1). It is a list of subjects, all stuffed to the point of bursting with materials deemed important by the respective subject specialists. Who do we suppose will take on the role of fulfilling all those other important aspirations? Which specialists are working to make the entire school a place with an intrinsic value? Or at least, What steps have been taken in the organization and design of the schools to accommodate this objective that everyone seems to agree is extremely important—at least, important enough for inclusion in the preamble to the act?

Which structures have been created to support its integration as a central component in the operation of the schools?

In my opinion, these aspirations have not been addressed, with the exception of a few dutiful nods of recognition in the preamble.

But others perceive the work of the National Curriculum Committee differently.

I will conclude this section with one such perception—here in the words of Torstein Harbo (1971, 58):[5]

> The two recommendations that we have been working on—the Preliminary Study for a National Curriculum for Compulsory Education and the Recommendation for a National Curriculum for Compulsory Education—are both the product of the past fifteen years' reformatory efforts, and the seeds of reformatory efforts to come. We are a modest nation far up in the North, and our resources are limited. Yet we have created a nine-year system of compulsory education equaling that of any other system in the world, in both organization and content. There is every reason to believe that our system will attract the attention of educators from around the world in the years to come.

## WATERTIGHT BULKHEADS

By assigning the school subjects a central and defining position, a large part of the school's organization is already set in stone. The situation is illustrated in figure 4.1. The student is at the bottom. Above them, forming a long, horizontal row, are the teachers of specific subjects. They are separated by watertight bulkheads. This layout is, of course, a direct reflection of the general principles already laid out by the national curriculum. Tear away the rosy picture and we discover a system staffed with individuals whose primary task it is to

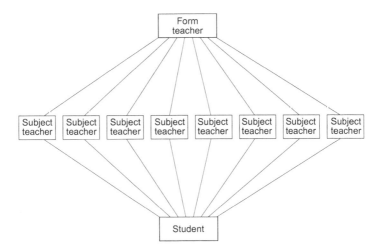

**Figure 4.1**   The basic organization of a Norwegian school.

communicate in detail the contents of their respective subjects. The only exception is the form teacher: situated above
the rest of the staff, the job of the form teacher is to coordinate the other teachers' schedules, contact parents, and
take care of the needs of individual students. The Regulatory
Committee for Primary and Lower Secondary Schools (1970,
131)—which we will shortly address in further detail—has
the following to say about the duties of the form teacher:

1. The form teacher's foremost responsibility is to help and
   guide students in their classes, both with regard to academic and social adjustment as well as questions or issues
   of a more personal nature. Of utmost importance is helping
   any students who are experiencing difficulties in school.
   The form teacher must endeavor to become apprised of
   the family life of each student, insofar as such knowledge
   may help in dealing with the student.

2. The form teacher is responsible for talking with students about their development and well-being at school, including being available for students during office hours.
3. The form teacher is responsible for overseeing the election of a chair, vice chair, and so on, including representatives for the student council where relevant. They are to serve as adviser for the student council and attend their meetings with the right to take the floor.

It all sounds promising—except that the Regulatory Committee seems to have forgotten that the form teacher is a subject-specific teacher just like the rest of the staff. The form teacher need not even be the teacher who spends the most time in the classroom.

A couple of years ago, I conducted a series of interviews with all the form teachers employed in a particular school district. The topic of the interviews concerned the relation between the form teachers and the students in their classes. The form teacher, I thought back then, would be the *generalist* of the school: they would *know* their class, be a stable ally, an adult with whom each student could have the closest form of contact. *But alas, most of the form teachers did not even know the names of all the students in their classes.* During the interviews, they were completely lost without their classroom rosters. And even with the roster placed in front of them, many struggled to recall who was who. The interviews took place at the end of the school year.

This doesn't mean that the form teachers were bad people—neither as human beings nor as teachers. It does, however, illustrate yet again the haphazard and outmoded way in which the schools have been organized in relation to and for the subjects. In-depth knowledge of a school subject requires specialization. The specialist cannot cover too many other subjects, so to fill their schedule they are made responsible for conveying their knowledge to many different classes. They are not permitted to linger for too long in the same place. This would make them less of a specialist in their area of expertise. Situated thus, at the center of everything, the subject-based system effectively obstructs the single premise that could enable a form teacher to function effectively.

In order to mitigate the adverse effects of the subject-based school, a series of *integration specialist* positions have been created. Here I am referring to "advisers" and "counselors." Among other things, counselors (Regulatory Committee, 1970, 134) are charged with the following:

Providing counsel on questions concerning further education and training, self-realization, and matters of social relations as well as other questions considered important by the student.

Helping students solve their personal as well as social difficulties and problems.

Documenting and recording needs for investigations, and treatment where necessary, as well as ensuring that students in need of help receive this.

The counselors (Regulatory Committee, 1970, 145) must "help students work out social difficulties and problems displayed in school [and] take preventive measures in the social sphere."

This may well be a reasonable scheme—given that the schools have been organized according to the subjects. But compared with the other option—the generalist (i.e., the form teacher)—the measures seem highly inadequate.

Especially in larger schools, it seems unlikely that such specialists will get to know any students other than those who cause the most trouble, much less be able intervene in the unobtrusive, day-to-day manner of the generalist.

We thus arrive at a tentative answer to the question of who holds power over the school: the *subjects* hold power over the school. They play an essential role in deciding what should take place, and how.


## THE INNER LIFE OF SCHOOLS

"The school is to promote intellectual freedom and tolerance, and endeavor to facilitate constructive modes of cooperation between teachers and students and between the school and the family." Thus sounded the autonomous and unambiguous will of the Norwegian Parliament. But it will not turn out that way if the Parliament allows its advisers to advise. The national curriculum—its subjects and testing systems—is reason enough. But the advice does not stop here.

Two committees were appointed to develop proposals on how to establish constructive modes of cooperation. First and foremost the Regulatory Committee was formed, inaugurated with a school inspector as its chair along with four additional educationists as ordinary members. The Regulatory Committee (1970) was charged with proposing regulations and providing standard guidelines for the inner life of schools. Shortly thereafter, another committee was created to carry out the task of providing more specific recommendations for how to structure the conditions for cooperation in schools. Their focus included all levels of schooling, and for this reason the committee's members represented other levels of schooling as well—including both parent and student representatives. The latter committee issued a brief and unwarranted recommendation on how to establish coordinating bodies in primary and secondary schools (Standing Committee on Cooperative Affairs, 1970). Its recommendation has been by and large incorporated into the Regulatory Committee's recommendation.

Both committees are determined to comply loyally with the intentions of Parliament. Cooperation should be initiated in all directions, from top to bottom. No less than ten smaller coordinating bodies are proposed, complete with standardized instructions for all of them:

1. *School council*—the chief municipal education officer as well as all principals and teachers employed on a full-time basis in each school district.
2. *Teachers' council*—all principals and teachers employed on a full-time basis at each school.
3. *Council for nonteaching personnel*—janitor, cleaning staff, school dentists and nurses, office employees, and so on.
4. *Class council, primary school*—elected student representatives from each class.
5. *Student council, primary school*—one representative and a potential alternate from each class, beginning in fourth grade.
6. *Class council, lower secondary school*—elected student representatives from each class.
7. *Student council, lower secondary school*—one representative and a potential alternate from each class, beginning in fourth grade.

8.  *General meeting*—for all students at a given school, teach-
    ers are entitled to participate.
9.  *Parents' council*—all parents or guardians of children in a
    given school.
10. *Liaison committee*—two representatives from the teach-
    ers' council, chair of the council for nonteaching person-
    nel (or a third party elected by its members), the school
    principal, two representatives from the lower secondary
    school student council, two representatives from the
    parents' council, and one representative chosen by the
    school board.

It is, by all means, an impressive machinery for cooperation. But it will never work. It cannot work because *the
machinery has nothing to work with.*

Let us take a closer look at two of the proposed councils—
that of the parents and the lower secondary school students.
We could have chosen any of the other councils. The principles at work are the same throughout. As for the parents'
council, its purpose according to the Regulatory Committee
(1970, 122) is to strengthen the bond between school and
family, foster the student's well-being and development, and
facilitate good contact between the school and society. A
little further down in the recommendation, their tasks are
specified in a bit more detail:

7.  By hosting meetings, get-togethers, and via other mea-
    sures, the working group for the parents' council must
    ensure that parents receive the information they need
    regarding both more general questions as well as those of
    special interest to the particular school.

8. In coordination with the school, the parents' council must take measures to promote sociopedagogical and recreational programs at the school.

9. The parents' council should address current matters relating to the entire school. The council should not consider issues pertaining to specific students nor directly intervene in day-to-day operations at the school.

10. The parents' council is to address matters presented by the liaison committee and school principal. (Regulatory Committee 1970, 123–124)

The alert reader may have noticed the absence of one particular word in the list of tasks. The word is "*DECIDE*." The parents' council is a body for orientation and deliberation. And even in conjunction with these matters, the council's influence is limited in that it is not permitted to discuss individual students or interfere with the daily operations of the school.

As with all the other proposed committees, the Standing Committee's (1970, 32–35) recommendation takes a much less restrictive approach. Among other things, it proposes that the following topics be addressed by the working group for the parents' councils:

School regulations

Allocation of the rooms of the school

The district's proposed school budget

Holidays and days off (school calendar)

Proposed changes in hours allocated to each school subject

Establishing or combining classes

The daily teaching hours

Length and time of recesses

School meal services
Traffic conditions and road safety around the school
School transportation and lodging
Safety and health-related initiatives for the students
Plans concerning repairs, renovation, and maintenance of
    school premises
Sociopedagogical initiatives

In addition, the recommendation notes that "the working group may establish direct contact with the school board's representative on the school's liaison committee. Should this representative be without a seat on the school board, the working group should ask their chair to request the right to participate and have a say on school board matters that involve the parents' council."

Although the parents' council is prevented from *deciding* anything, it at least now has a seat on another body—namely, the proposed liaison committee. But if we were to subject this to scrutiny, we would find once again only proposals for nonbinding *statements*—with one exception. Both the Regulatory Committee and Standing Committee on Cooperative Affairs propose that on "approval of the school board, the council can, in certain cases, be granted decision-making authority." Which cases this would imply remains unspecified. Nor are there any reflections of this proposal in the provisions stipulating the duties of the school board.

As for the lower secondary school student councils—according to the recommendation from the Regulatory Committee (1970, 119–120)—they must promote the common interests of the school's students and follow up on the work done by the class councils to create a harmonious school community. The Standing Committee on Cooperative Affairs (1970, 7) opted for brisker wording. Instead of "harmony," it proposed that the student councils work toward creating a "thriving school community." A memo from the Regulatory Committee specifies its work tasks:

> The student council must serve as a unifying body for all students at the school. Therefore, it must refrain from engaging in the creation of resolutions or other forms of political or ideological activity. In coordination with its contact teacher/activity leader and the principal, the council should establish the foundation for the creation of student societies, clubs, study groups, and other activity groups at the school.

As should be evident by now, the Standing Committee on Cooperative Affairs is a bit bolder. It agrees that the student council should neither engage in the work of resolutions nor in political or ideological activities, but adds that "questions concerning school politics should, however, be addressed by the student council and in coordination with the contact teacher/activity leader and the principal, the student council should establish the foundation for the creation of student societies, clubs, study groups, and other activity groups at the school." Both committees agree that any "initiative proposed by the student council must first be approved by the principal."

What the proposed councils all have in common is that they are overcontrolled and underemployed. The details of their work and how they should carry it out are determined by others, from the outside. And as if this weren't enough, these others have decided that they aren't going to decide anything. They must issue advice. Talk.

But we do know a thing or two about social life. We happen to know that social life functions according to some specific premises. As organisms, human beings are rational in their actions. Or they are, at least, *also* rational. They do not gather voluntarily unless they have something to give or there is some benefit to be derived from their being together. Parents are no different.

In his now-seminal analysis of the village of Hilltown, George Homans (1951) illustrates how community life withers when decision-making powers are taken out of the hands of the community.[6] There was once an important value ascribed to the prefatory discussions held on the street corner, at the store in the evenings, and finally at the city council meetings. These arenas played a key role in deciding how to spend the community's resources, where to construct wells and new roads, the location of the school, and how teaching should be carried out inside it. Important, provocative, conflict-inducing questions. People loathed one another those days. Skipping a meeting was out of the question because some outrageous decision might be made. But people were passionate about supporting their friends, and for that reason, were always around. Always, that is, until the day arrived when there was nothing real left to talk about.

And this was exactly what happened the day that Hilltown lost control of its own destiny. This was what happened once each and every important decision was made *outside* Hilltown. This was what happened once Hilltown was integrated into the greater society, where decisions on the construction and maintenance of roads were made by the Public Roads Administration, the local water supplies were connected to the state's waterworks, and the church was run on external financing—and the school was subjugated to external powers. And just like that, people stopped gathering in the store in the evenings. Just like that, the local community suddenly became too tired to attend any more city council meetings. Convincing people to show up became an arduous task. They thought only of themselves and were unwilling to sacrifice anything for the community. They were rational beings; they knew all too well that their presence didn't matter anyway. But I guess we all know this. So too do the members of the Regulatory Committee and Standing Committee on Cooperative Affairs. They do not participate anymore than others unless they somehow find it to be of significance.

Social organizations need sustenance. There are two common types of such sustenance. The first is access to important information that cannot be procured through other means. The second is power. There is little to suggest that any of the councils proposed above will be given either. The liaison committee will waste away. And the skeptics will receive confirmation: the students are too immature, and the parents are too unwilling to participate in the life of the school. It would be best if schools were run by the educationists.[7]

It would be best, this is true, as long as the fundamental premises remain unchanged. And neither the Norwegian Parliament, Regulatory Committee, nor Standing Committee on Cooperative Affairs express any inclination to make such changes. But if the school is to nurture cooperation, it must be granted dominion over its own life.

## POWER OVER SCHOOLS

The problem stems from the fact that both the Parliament and the writers of regulations are trying to achieve two things at once. The two things they are trying to achieve cannot coexist. On the one hand, they want to create a thriving school community, which is both beneficial and important. There is no cause to doubt the sincerity of their intentions in this regard. But they also want something else. They want to preserve the main characteristics of the existing organization of schools. And not only do they want to preserve it, they want expand its inherent idiosyncrasies along the same lines.

From the perspective of the students, it probably appears as if it is the teacher who reigns over the school. For the teacher, it appears as if it is the school principal. But the principal knows all too well that it is the chief municipal education officer, who knows that it is the board of education—whose members know, or at least suspect, that it is someone even higher up. Figure 4.2 presents an approximate image of the order of things. A quick glance should be enough to see the main point: the school is constructed as a profoundly hierarchical system. Between a single student and the highest authority there are at least ten agencies. Many more could have been listed. Municipal executives, the council for primary and lower secondary education, head teachers, and advisers are all to be found somewhere in between the student and the uppermost agency. Anyone seeking to travel through the system would be in for a long journey. But the diagram also illustrates another important point.

In a system replete with dignitaries, all of whom want to have a say, little remains to be shared with the newcomers.

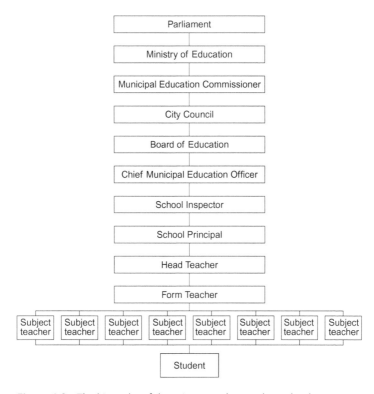

**Figure 4.2**  The hierarchy of the primary and secondary school system.

And if there is nothing to be shared, even parents lose their rights. Having little left, the *school principal* simply has no authority to bestow on the parents council. All matters of importance have either been decided in advance—the curriculum, length of the school year, schedule, lesson plans, and so on—or are decided by others, as in the case of the school's budget, the hiring of teachers, or further expansions of the school. Principals administrate teachers inside the school. They file *recommendations* with the higher authorities. And they can grant their teachers a leave of absence for no more than three days and their students for up to six days. But beyond these measures, they are first and foremost there to ensure that instructions are followed, and discipline and order prevail. Because they did well as a teacher, they have advanced to the role of supervisor on level five of the ladder.

*The chief municipal education officer* is there to keep the principal in check. According to the standard instructions offered by the Regulatory Committee (140–141), the chief municipal education officer must

> ensure that the school is run according to the approved objectives and the most current laws, and in compliance with the provisions found in the curriculum, school regulations, and guidelines, and so on. ... In accordance with the decisions of the school board, he is responsible for allocating the school's budget and acquisitions. Each school principal is to be held accountable by the chief municipal education officer for management of the budget. He must ensure the disbursement of resources in a manner that is expedient and economical. ... He can close the school for a given number of hours or days. He can grant students a leave of absence for up to two weeks.

But above the chief municipal education officer is *the board of education*. The board "ensures that the school is run in accordance with the prevailing laws and regulations and municipal resolutions, and makes sure that the composition of the teaching staff is expedient in terms of the subjects to be taught, and that the school satisfies the prevailing requirements at any given time" (Primary and Lower Secondary Education Act, Section 26).

What follows is the creation of new positions, and subsequent to that, proposals for the school budget and potential expansions.

But the board of education must function in relation to not one but two superiors: the city council and the *municipal education commissioner*. As stated by the Regulatory Committee (105–106), the board of education must provide the commissioner with the following materials:

- A copy of the minutes from the most recent board meeting, no more than a week after the meeting has been held (L Section 27.9).

- For cases requiring special attention by an approving body, a copy of the notes must be appended. Suggested division of school classes (L Section 5.7).

- Suggestions on the organization of subjects and the school schedule, and lesson plans including guidelines and appendixes (L Section 7; Section 11).

- Decisions on the dates of school holidays and breaks during the school year (R Section 3).

- Applications for approval of school transportation arrangements (R Section 1).

- Appointment of staff members, announcements concerning short-term contracts, and decisions concerning full-time employment and the period of employment (L Section 18; Section 20).

- Applications for leave (L Section 18).

- Announcements concerning resignations and terminations.

- Announcements concerning the approval of new textbooks, ABC books, and reading materials to be introduced (L Section 40)—and concerning the language of instruction (L Section 41).[8]

- Announcements concerning deaf, blind, or mentally disabled children, children with speech, reading, or writing difficulties, and children with mental health issues or other disabilities.

- Suggestions for district changes, including the choice of a new location for the school (L Section 3).

- Blueprints for school buildings and student housing, plans for new buildings or reconstruction of the existing school and student housing, and plans for the design of outdoor areas with playgrounds (L Section 9).

- Applications for pilot schemes in schools (cf. the act concerning pilot schemes in schools).

- Estimates of expenses eligible for state subsidies (L Section 39).

- Tasks related to reimbursement of expenses from state subsidies in accordance with the provisions on state subsidies (L Section 39).[9]

On behalf of the Standing Committee on Education and Church Affairs, the municipal commissioner of education must "ensure compliance with all regulations pertaining to the primary and lower secondary school in legal documents, regulations, and guidelines, directives, and so on. ... The commissioner has the right to attend and speak at district meetings and meetings of the school boards, the city council, the county school board, and in the county parliament when school-related matters are under consideration" (Regulatory Committee, 136).

Put simply, there is no room for more people. Just about everything has already been decided by laws, regulations, lesson plans, the curriculum, and examination requirements. Any further decisions that remain to be made have been so carefully dispensed to so many hierarchically situated agencies as to effectively remove any form of sustenance for the inner life of schools. The ten proposed coordinating councils will become nothing but pale shadows. Their members will know that things are actually being decided elsewhere. They will know where things are truly happening—that is, in places where they are not invited. So they may as well stay home.

Expanding the size of the agencies works in a similar fashion. In a small municipality, the need for administration will be kept at a minimum. The Board of Education would, perhaps, have no more than a single school to administer. And if the board members have children of compulsory school age, they would be enrolled in that school. The roles of board member and parent melt into one. If the school is small enough, the intermediary roles of head teacher and deputy head also become redundant. The same goes for form teachers and school principals. The municipal commissioner of education would be shared by several municipalities. Most matters would still be decided elsewhere, but at least the distance from the top to the bottom of the system would be reduced.

But this is far from the reality in most municipalities—and less and less so all the time. The agencies continue to grow. The organizational hierarchy is mobilized from top to bottom. The distance increases not just from top to bottom but also between each agency. Most evident is the gap between the individual school and board of education. In Oslo alone there are fifty-seven primary schools, twelve combined primary and lower secondary schools, and sixteen lower secondary schools. Combined, they constitute a student body of almost fifty thousand. In addition to this there are vocational and academic upper secondary schools, institutions of higher learning, and so on. Not only have decisions been taken out of the hands of the individual schools. Now they are being made by strangers. Little can be done to impede such forces.

Another consequence—feeding the growth of the agencies—is the expanding power of the permanent employees within the administration. The sheer size of the system requires that still more time be spent on maintaining oversight. Amateurs are obliged to delegate more and more of their authority. As the number of intermediaries in the bureaucracy increases, so too does the number of administrative staff positioned somewhere above the publicly elected representatives—providing yet another reason to stay silent and let the professionals do the talking. The amateurs, for their own part, must then also try to become permanent specialists. The Oslo school board has twelve subcommittees attending to various tasks. In addition to the hierarchical structure, the school board—much like the school—thus becomes an organization based on specialization.

Many publicly elected representatives dream about a smaller system in which proximity and transparency replace specialization and bureaucracy. But they have both wage regulations and other internal growth factors against them. The larger the school, the more money the school principal makes, and the less available time there is for them to do any teaching. The same holds true for rectors and the administrators of schools for children with learning disabilities. To employ a head teacher, the school must be of a certain size. And the larger the municipal school system—measured as the total number of teaching hours in the municipality— the greater the administration's salaries. Any person who is deliberately working to share their school or district with others would be an unselfish person indeed.

Large agencies are a good fit in terms of the other needs of the school system as a whole. Many have ambitions to make something of their lives. Often, these ambitions are synonymous with ascending through the ranks. A ladder with many rungs provides many people with the opportunity for upward mobility and a few with the possibility of making it all the way to the top. And so we once again find a harmonious correspondence between the school and the overall structure of society. We live in a stratified society that is mirrored in the inner structure of our schools. The educationists are no different from other people. There are, therefore, plentiful forces within the system pushing to create even greater distance between the ranks.

The organization of schools is a reflection of the surrounding society. And while this organization of the school's inner life makes it impossible to achieve other important objectives, there is little doubt as to which forces predominantly hold sway in the current situation. The inner life of schools parallels the common ways in which we organize ourselves as a society. And as long as schools satisfy their other primary functions of storage and certification, they are left in peace. Lindbekk (1971, 15) expresses amazement about how seldom the school is subjected to any scrutiny:

> And the most peculiar aspect of the institution/society relation—at least with regard to the school—is how little the

surrounding society and its institutions actually seem to care, how rarely they place the products of schools under scrutiny, how rarely we see feedback from the consumer to the producer, and how rarely the recipients of the schools' output raise the all-important question, Is this output worth its investment—that is, the money that we, the recipients, channel toward the school through taxation, duties, and so on?

I agree with his observation, but not his sense of surprise. Only rarely do the school's recipients, society, ask such significant questions. But that is presumably because schools are effective at delivering their services. This is also why I disagree with Lindbekk (1971, 15) when he goes on to say that "from this perspective, the most astonishing fact about our school system is the degree to which this vast institutional apparatus has succeeded in detaching itself from the rest of society." This is, once again, only partially true. As illustrated in this chapter, the school does have a relatively large degree of autonomy. I have a strong suspicion, however, that this condition would be difficult to maintain the moment the school *ceased* to align itself so seamlessly with the principal structures of society and ceased to deliver the goods in demand by that society. The moment a school might venture to rattle its chains in such a way, the nature of those chains would become apparent for all to see. The entrenchment of schools in the order of things would be dragged out into the light of day. And we would realize—because the issue concerns a profession with comparatively low degrees of specialization—the defenselessness of schools in the face of pressure from the surrounding society. Such an opinion does not imply that we are powerless when it comes to implementing any changes. The next chapter is full of suggestions for change. But the odds are against us.

It has become a hierarchically structured system controlled chiefly by educationists. But it was not intended as
such. During the previous century's struggles for municipal
self-governance, the school was a key issue. The municipalities and especially parents were to be granted full authority
over their own schools. Their struggle was initially successful. Once control over the municipalities had been placed in
the hands of the people in 1884, control over the schools followed suit, on the force of the Education Act of 1889 (*folkeskoleloven*). Under the subtitle *A Growing Opposition's Ideals*,
Dokka (1967, 407) writes,

> The underlying idea of the initial program for public schools
> was that parents should maintain the rights and responsibil-
> ity concerning their children's education and upbringing. The
> key points of the Education Act of 1889 were based on this
> fundamental idea. Parental rights were the chief reason why
> the school was placed under municipal authority to such a
> large degree. In principle, the intention was to grant parents
> the right to choose the kind of education and upbringing their
> children would receive. The selection of teachers and deter-
> mination of teaching objectives therefore became municipal
> tasks. The school was governed by the people because it was
> considered to be the responsibility of parents.

In the second-to-last chapter of his opus on the historical
foundations of the Norwegian public school, Dokka (1967,
409) goes on to add,

> Through the implementation of the municipal reform (whereby
> control of the municipal government was devolved into the
> hands of the people in 1884), the path had been cleared for
> the chief aspect of the program for public schools—that is,
> that the school should be run by the people and should be their
> responsibility. Only then would the school be worthy of a free

people. Only then would it be able to fulfill its promise in a free society.

But the seeds preventing Dokka's descriptions from ever being realized had already been sown many years before by the first administrator to enter the Norwegian school system. They were sown through the Education Act of 1860 (*Lov om Allmueskolevæsenet på landet*), concerning the establishment of the rural public school system, when for the first time positions for municipal education commissioners were established. Some resisted, though. Dokka (1967, 181) writes that

> especially [Søren Pedersen] Jaabæk expressed concern about the impact of newly established public offices on the continued growth of the public school.[10] Their introduction would result in such reinforcement and centralization of the overall administration, such an expansion of a clerical hierarchy with authority over the municipal school system, that there was every reason to fear the development of an increasingly uniform school.

Yet as so many times before, Jaabæk's concerns were ignored.

It should, by now, be increasingly apparent why this book opened with a section about a French village, followed by a section about the conditions of the Sioux people's school, and a section about life in a British lower secondary school. But I will put my pointer away. Let us instead approach our topic from a wholly different angle. So far, we have limited our scope to what *is*. Let us, in an attempt toward liberation, now turn toward an exploration of what *could be*.

# 5

# A DIFFERENT SCHOOL

If people really believed that the world was controlled by forces external to themselves, they probably wouldn't write books—perhaps with the exception of those who felt pressured by those forces to write them. I, for one, do not feel pressured. On the contrary, I believe and hope that the perspectives I have presented above will have a disruptive impact on society's predominant solutions. I have faith, without doubt due to my sociological common sense, in the transformative power of thoughts. At least, that is, if these thoughts are expressed at more or less the right time. But perhaps sociology may also prove valuable in helping us understand how thoughts acquire influence. We have moved far beyond the village school, but continue to struggle with its fundamental structure. The result is a school based on stratification, a school that is suitable for upholding both a class structure and its own function as a storage space. But our society is evolving, however. Alternative solutions become more and more evident—with time they are visible to everyone, and perhaps a bit too visible for some. On reaching middle age we tend to exaggerate the beauty of childhood, the charm of youth, though perhaps this response is not as given as we might believe it to be. It is possible that we needed a storage space or the commonly defended stratification service provided by schools. Yet for all these supposedly necessary school services—although I would have preferred other approaches—they have failed to hinder the perhaps most central thing: we have become satiated. Social inequality remains. A society divided by social classes is flourishing with increasing fervor. The internal inequalities have presumably increased. At many workplaces, life has become even more exhausting. Nevertheless, crucial changes must have taken place in that more immediate material needs no longer threaten Norway as they did in the past. These changes should remind us that there *is* a difference between relative and absolute suffering. A hundred years ago, one-fourth of the population died before reaching adulthood. An additional fourth never married, while those who did could only afford this luxury after they turned thirty. Compared to our past, we are free. With greater certainty of sufficient material resources than any society ever before, we are able to sit back, look at our lives, and reflect on our own handiwork.

But more than this—and this is where the sociological common sense comes in again—the liberation from the most elementary material suffering has given rise to other needs (whether they are articulated or just experienced) that will most likely affect the situation for schools as well. You don't scream for more food when your mouth is full. Our technologies have been immensely successful. We can now produce *things*. Other aspects, however, are still in need of attention. I have tried to put into words what these *other aspects* are, but have given up; they are not easily captured by words.

Perhaps it will suffice to state that these aspects involve ways of living together, ways of living *beyond* the satisfaction of material needs, ways of living that affect both those who live together and those who live alone. The current young generation—satiated through and through in terms of its material needs—are the most apparent apostles and in most apparent need of a different school. The question is whether there should be a school at all.

Schools are mirrors of society. It is thus society that must be changed first, some claim. I would warmly welcome such changes. But if we believe in the power of thought—and thus believe that schools are more than mirrors—it seems only reasonable to attempt to promote change on several fronts at the same time. This chapter takes a step in this direction. I will begin with the minor reforms and then gradually proceed to the more substantial issues. First, though, something must be said about the cul-de-sacs in the landscape.

## CUL-DE-SACS

*"If only we had better teachers."*

I cannot imagine a more futile starting point for educational reform. We *have* excellent teachers—as good as the ordinary run of Norwegians, although their capabilities are, presumably, even a bit better. A disproportionate number come from middle-class backgrounds, and are from villages and above all western Norway.[1] On the whole, this may lead to entire generations of teachers who will be slightly out of sync with the values of the children and young people who are born in cities. It would not hurt to include more working-class teachers, more teachers who thought with their hands and not their heads, and more teachers who come from some of the more underdeveloped regions of Norway. Yet this is of little importance. And it seems unlikely that this is what people have in mind when they call for better teachers. What they are calling for is rather, "We need those who are equipped to deal with children and young people." But then we find ourselves immediately in the vicinity of the important questions, Which children, and to what ends? I wonder if many of the teachers who are suffering today—or let others suffer under their control—would have functioned *better* if only the objectives and frameworks had been of a different nature. My optimistic guess is that *most* teachers are equipped to deal with children and young people—at least if they are allowed to do what both parties find important. But it does not make any real difference if I am wrong. Children are so numerous and different, and their transition to adult life so problematic, that any notion of an elitist selection of teachers is out of the question. We must adapt conditions to accommodate an average capacity and then factor deviations (both below and above) into the equation.

*"But they should have better working conditions so that the most qualified candidates would apply."*

More money—surely this wouldn't hurt. Whether those who want to make a lot of money are also those who are best qualified to deal with children remains an open question, though. The same holds true for another common demand with an eye to improving conditions: fewer children in each classroom. It seems likely—although not certain—that lower student-teacher ratios would be more comfortable. But this would also give the authority figure in the room more power and time to impart the curriculum to the students. And what if the curriculum is irrelevant or perhaps even harmful? What if the teacher's increased freedom and resources led to even stricter performance requirements?

*"But the architecture of schools should be changed."*

I certainly wouldn't mind. And it *is* good that something is happening.[2] The open schools that are attracting so much attention these days represent an exciting step forward, making possible both large and small spaces that can be adapted to class sizes as well as adjusted to a variety of subjects, working methods, and group compositions. These changes represent a great and by all means timely development in light of the thoughtless monuments that have been constructed up to now. But they represent only a small fragment of the larger mosaic of important things that must be changed. It would be a perilous path to follow if in applying so much thought and faith to opening up the interior of buildings, we neglected to take into account that the external walls remained intact. What's more, this open architecture can provide teachers with even better opportunities to impart the knowledge stipulated by the traditional requirements of the school as well as ensure that both they and their colleagues are diligent in their compliance with the same. "Open schools" may be open for both good and evil.

We must dig deeper.

## A FREE SCHOOL COMMUNITY

First and foremost, let us take the preamble seriously! Let us take the *entire* preamble seriously, not solely the part about knowledge. In chapter 4, I already pointed out some of its most apparent limitations. Let me now, in the spirit of a proposal, elaborate on the consequences of these.

If our mission is to create a thriving school community of collaborating individuals, the first requirement must be to do away with the system's structure of a giant stepladder with a control center dictating activities from above. There is only one way to do this. Ripping off the bandage will hurt. But only in the beginning.

We must do the exact opposite of what everyone is demanding. *We must cut down on administration*. We must first of all cut down on the control center's external management of schools. We must work from the top down, and strip away a number of the Ministry of Education and Church Affair's mandates for the schools. We must become free *from*—and hereby free *to*. Next in line would be the abolition of established positions such as municipal education commissioners. And we must get rid of—or if that isn't possible, then at least downgrade—all remaining parts of the school administration so that their power and authority equals that of the teachers. Alternatively, we could work toward elevating the power and authority (and status) of the teachers in order to place them on equal footing with the present administration. It is, in a sense, insignificant which strategy is chosen. The main point is to establish a situation—a system—where all important decisions are made within or in close proximity to each individual school. If the school community is to be a thriving and significant entity, its most vital and essential decisions cannot be made by those seated on the top floor.

This, of course, would be madness. At least, that is, in the minds of the already-weary office managers, division heads, municipal education commissioners, chief municipal education officers, and school inspectors who spend their days drowning in paperwork—letters to be answered, projects to be coordinated, and decisions to be made. It would be chaos—half measures, solutions at cross-purposes, and half-baked, scandalous solutions. *I* know it too. The solution I propose does not come without a cost. It would not result in *similar* schools offering the same quality education throughout the country—at least not similar in terms of the notion of the uniform *quality* currently envisioned by district commissioners. On the other hand, the impact of the variation would not only be negative. It would be a matter of variation, or for better or worse, a "natural experiment" of sorts, and thereby most likely a speedier rate of renewal for the school system.

Our current centralized, top-down governed system ensures justice in the sense that everyone is guaranteed similarity. But this also means restraint when faced with trying new solutions, and a sluggish pace in their implementation. In the current framework, introducing or removing a novel solution is a case of all or nothing at all; new solutions must always involve the system as a whole. And if the solution turns out to be a mistake, it will be removed in its entirety. This structure, which seems so obvious, would enable the central authorities to ensure that the nation's schools are constantly up to date and in a position to benefit from the best educational advancements. Yet this is not how centralized decision making works. It follows its own laws. It requires accountability and simplified decision-making procedures. The more power the system has, the less reason its administrators have to take any initiative. The flow of inquiries forces them to make decisions *concerning what other people ask about.* They acquire the role of a court of law. There are strong forces at work that are impeding these agencies from experimentation or even being close to the centers of activity.[3]

And even if I am wrong—even if an external administration played an instrumental role in realizing the lofty visions for our schools—I would nevertheless insist on the necessity of *cutting down at the top.* Most social schemes come at a cost. Even if a centralized decision-making body were advantageous for the educational system as a whole, any benefits would be outweighed by the inherent disadvantages it entails for the individual schools. If students, together with the teachers, together with the parents, are to realize the ambition of a thriving school community, we must first abandon the belief that centralization is beneficial.

*"But won't this just lead to more power for principals and head teachers?"*

Certainly. That is why *they must also be cut.* We must once again consciously try to counteract the built-in tendencies of social organisms to establish pyramid structures in which all power—along with honors and payment—is situated at the top. By design, we must counteract the creation of more head teacher posts and try to do away with existing ones. Higher salaries must be negotiated and awarded on the basis of criteria other than specialization. The same goes for the role of principal. Managing other teachers is not a job worthy of any self-respecting educator, and even less so the misguided practice of assigning such a task to our best educators. Besides, such a position is downright harmful if the preamble is to be taken seriously. Abolishing the administrative authority as such would compel other solutions to emerge. Some schools would, perhaps, fall back on appointing a principal. Others would prefer collective decision making. Others would choose anarchy. A wealth of experience demonstrates that most people manage to find a way to function if they need to, if they are left to their own devices. In such instances, the search in its own right for this way of functioning would become one of the main purposes of the school—that is, learning to function as a community through life experience.

I do not see a need to cut down on the number of form teachers, since they seldom exercise any power, but something must be done about the subject-specific teachers. Today, the imaginary silos of each teacher's subject continue to determine why our curriculum becomes a curriculum. If we are to create a school community with room for something other than isolated subjects, we cannot staff the community with people who are first and foremost there for their *subject*. School communities must primarily be made up of specialized generalists who are able to navigate diversity. Edvard Befring has suggested calling these individuals general education professionals, and these participants must be prioritized, for a while at least, since the importance of their role seems to have been completely forgotten. Later we can begin to ponder the significance of subjects such as math and history.

In line with this, I see no need to cut down on the teachers' resource centers, councils, and minor committees, insofar, that is, as they serve only as coordinating agencies that give *advice*—and nothing more. They will doubtless be heard should they come up with something wise.

*"But does that mean that school communities should govern themselves?"*

Yes. And in keeping with this, yet another agency must be shut down: the board of education. The school boards were created for the previous generation, not ours. They were created for small schools in small communities where everyone knew one another. In such cases, everyone knew who the best-qualified professionals were, where and how these individuals could be influenced to become even better qualified, and thereby create an even better school.

Why not try to re-create this situation? Once again, some people are already working toward this goal. The solution must replicate the one proposed for the centralized administration: we must curtail the influence of the current boards of education. We must absolve them of their duties and authority, and return these to the schools. This almost came to pass in the last century. But the change was not implemented, in part due to a widespread anxiety that the church would hereby gain too much influence over local committees. This anxiety should be less relevant today, and the arguments for reassigning tasks and power to the schools have become considerably stronger. A single board for all the schools in a single district can only generate alienation, internal specialization, and an inevitable release of power into the hands of the central administration.

Why not rob from the board of education and channel the funds to the dozens of school councils proposed by the Regulatory Committee and Standing Committee on Cooperative Affairs, taking care to redistribute more than mere ornamentation? We must redistribute the *important* decisions. If a district has a budgeted amount to spend on its schools, it should be possible to distribute this amount among the schools according to some kind of principle. It would then be up to each particular school to decide how the money should be spent. It is not difficult to imagine the uproar that would ensue in response to such a redistribution model: it would be madness. How would it be managed? And who would decide? Some schools would fall into neglect. It would be unjust and, above all, irresponsible.

There are two types of answers for the question of who ought to have decision-making authority. One type of answer is to produce regulations that will determine this. This answer is similar to the idea of an administrator who will be the school's final authority. The other type of answer is more in keeping with the ideas of this book: the individual school—along with the people who voluntarily run the school, or that is, the parents—should decide who will have decision-making authority. And the deliberations about this—about whom, what, and how—would be among the most significant struggles in the life of the school, during the first year and all the years to come.

At the risk of jumping the gun on some of the suggestions offered on the following pages, let me try to be as specific as possible. Schools should have the power to make decisions about their own budgets. They should decide for themselves whether they wish to renovate buildings, build a laboratory in the woodworking shop, create a skating rink, or perhaps sacrifice earthly conveniences and take all seventh graders on a field trip to Svalbard. All this would probably be expensive. But what if they chose *not* to fill the vacant position after old Bob retired? Why on earth shouldn't this decision belong to the school itself?

And then there is the question of employment. Today, teachers apply for positions throughout the entire district before being assigned to particular schools by the board of education. Some principals, the best ones, probably have more direct contact with the school board and its administration than others. They are probably able to attract the teachers they find to be best suited for the policy of what is, quite literally, "their" school. These principals are presumably quite satisfied with the way things are. It seems that change, in most systems, occurs slowly, simply because a select group of individuals benefits from the current system. But somebody loses out. It would be better if schools were allowed to procure the staff they needed through direct contact and hiring. This could produce dynamic communities competing to create and offer the best possible working environments. In some instances, this liberty should not be absolute. Perhaps the district's central administration should have some say in the decision making, such as the decision to reassign particularly qualified teachers to exceptionally difficult positions. Given the class-specific nature of housing patterns, some districts would be less attractive than others. It might be the case that such leveling mechanisms would be in order—although I doubt this would really be necessary as long as the rest of the items on my wish list are granted.

## AN OPEN CURRICULUM

It is not enough to tear down the control centers. The directives must also be removed. From a historical perspective, the national curriculum is a young phenomenon, and we should take care to ensure it does not grow old.

This does not imply the end of lesson plans altogether. *Many* people, with different backgrounds and qualifications, should participate in the creation of lesson plans, and the existing proposals can serve as a kind of initial blueprint, but to be read as inspiring catalysts rather than directives for action. The deliberations involved when choosing among these temptations must constitute the core contents of each individual school community. This point, of course, would imply the end of nationally standardized exams. Any praise of self-rule and decentralization will be empty words as long as the central governing authorities continue to impose the same standards on all the schools. Exams do not simply test students: they also test teachers and, in a sense, the overall quality of the school in relation to the centrally determined learning objectives. The national exam is what ensures that the reins of power over schooling stay firmly in the hands of the central authorities.

As this book goes to press, the Ministry of Education and Church Affairs in Norway has outlined its proposal for Curriculum Guidelines for Compulsory Education (1971), which builds on the recommendations of the National Curriculum Committee. To some extent, it is an attempt to lessen the pressure of each specific subject. In lower secondary school, one hour a week is allocated to class and student council activities. Furthermore, math has been made an elective in the ninth grade—although math competence remains one of the criteria for admission to upper secondary school. Nor is there any clarity with regard to examinations. "An assessment of a student's proficiency in different subjects should never be a one-sided determination of the student's skills and achievements" (Curriculum Guidelines for Compulsory Education, 1971, 59). On the other hand, what follows is a virtually verbatim rendering of the National Curriculum Committee's Recommendation II regarding how "it is indispensable to disclose information about a student's assessed attainment in their transition from compulsory schooling to working life or further education." And

> it will generally be necessary to develop specific sets of questions, assignments, exercises or the like when the purpose of an assessment is to try to determine students' actual levels of proficiency in different subjects. These questions are also important for a number of other assessments. Advice is therefore found in the lesson plans on how to produce such resources, which are to be made available as publicly accessible documents, and may be used when deemed expedient for the assessment in question. This applies to both the assessment of skills and achievements as well as abilities and talents. (59)

It doesn't help much to state that the Curriculum Guidelines "must not be understood as binding minimum requirements for all students" (24) if at the same time a system of control is established whereby those who have fulfilled the most requirements also perform best. The wording of the Curriculum Guidelines is generally much more cautious than that of the national curriculum. Moreover, the Curriculum Guidelines contain a wealth of perspectives regarding the importance of learning how to *find* knowledge rather than simply *knowing* it. Something—or someone—is carefully moving us away from a comprehensive, subject-based school system. This is stated with even greater clarity in the press release that followed the publication of the new Curriculum Guidelines for Compulsory Education.[4]

Would not abandoning a system that ensures common academic standards with centralized exams ruin the possibility of controlling student admissions to both upper secondary and tertiary educations?

Exactly—and this is one of the greatest benefits of the suggested reform. A vagueness would be introduced, and perhaps even uncertainty concerning those supposedly best fit for pursuing higher education and certain professions. To read the history of the public school is to read a saga of slavery. Over and over again—and through disparate means—the slave and their companions struggle to rise to the level of a gentleman, the one who administers knowledge and culture, and knows how everything must be. And if mandatory attendance at the peasants' school—or *people's* school, as it was deftly named to skirt the connotations of slavery—was extended in its duration, the best students could perhaps even be allowed to continue their studies at an upper secondary school. If the days were longer, if the year was longer, if the number of years was increased—it would be a school to the gentleman's satisfaction. Meanwhile, if tougher requirements were imposed, the national curriculum expanded, nationwide exams introduced, and of course, a couple of additional ploys executed along the way, signals of reassurance would be sent to the gentlemen that even though this is a school for everyone, differences will still be upheld. Thus came the lesson plans or the series of schemes designed to prevent those deemed most unfit from attending the people's school (or in any case, to expel them as quickly as possible in the event they had somehow landed there by mistake). This would please the gentlemen and they might even venture to send their own children to the school.

And so the school continues its acts of slave-like submission, blissfully unaware that the battle has already been won. The victory stems not from the school's own achievements but instead from the fact that the outer circumstances no longer require slave-like submission. Several factors in the mix conspire to ensure this: in some schools, no more than half the student body continues on to upper secondary school. If more were to do so, the upper secondary schools would lose a lot of their power, and increasingly adapt themselves so as to take what they could get. No one really believes that upper secondary schools in Oslo would stop admitting students even if the lower secondary schools stopped teaching German or other foreign languages in addition to English. Upper secondary schools would not stop admitting students even if the lower secondary schools stopped teaching English, botany, mathematics, and chemistry. The upper secondary schools must take what they can get because they depend on their students. They will have to adapt. All that is required is to set the wheels in motion.

Other schools, however, have no troubles filling up their rosters. In such cases, it is easy to see why primary schools end up submitting to the whims of the higher levels. This submission is, nevertheless, unnecessary. As will become still clearer for everyone, most of what is stated in this book about primary and lower secondary schools also applies to upper secondary schools. This will soon become clear to everyone, and the upper secondary schools will begin to unravel from the inside out. Once the Parliament realizes that external circumstances have eliminated the need for submission, it will try to open up the system from above. The universities are well aware of these changing circumstances and are in the process of creating exactly these openings.

There are, of course, many pawns in the game. Secondary schools have slaved to satisfy *their* master. That is, the alma mater, the overseer of the real and distant truths—and the cradle of teachers for our secondary schools. And yet it is exactly from this level that we now can deal the critical blow to the secondary school's power over primary and lower secondary schools. Increasingly, secondary school diplomas will no longer serve as the only certificate qualifying students for admission to higher education. There is a visible trend in a number of industrialized countries that resembles that of the distant socialist countries: admission to universities can and should be recruited directly from the people. A discussion of why this practice is flourishing at this moment, how justified it is, or whether it is good or bad in the long run is beyond the scope of this book. We must be satisfied by simply stating that such a trend *does* exist, and then ask what it means for the position of upper secondary schools. The more this trend catches on, the more these schools will lose their monopoly. They will thereby also be relieved of a burden. They too will be freed from their master. They will be free to cooperate with their equals in the primary and lower secondary schools—free to fully receive what these schools have to offer.

## SCHOOLS AND THE DIVISION INTO CLASSES

But alas, we must not forget the lessons learned in chapter 3! One of the main points was that schools provide a service in the name of class distinctions. If the system was opened up in such a way as to grant everyone free access everywhere, then it would not be possible to carry out this service. Make up your mind, man! Are we supposed to follow the advice of chapter 3 or chapter 5?

Both. Chapter 3 described the place of schools within the class structure as well as the service that the school has provided up to now and chiefly still supplies. But ours is not a completely static society. Several circumstances have begun impeding the ability of schools to provide class certification. First, there are so many who attend school for so many years that the pyramid is becoming heavy at the top. We have reached a certain saturation point. We cannot assign power and honor to so many. When being posh is normalized, it ceases to be desirable. The saturation point will be reached if a large percentage of the population pursues an education until they are twenty-five to thirty years old. Increasing numbers decrease the value of each degree, so the declining status of students is not only a matter of radicalism. And having spent so many years in school, in the end it almost seems comical—and a silly waste of time—if someone tries to ascend through education to a rank above others.

Doubt acquires fertile growing conditions when more and more people are snooping around inside the temples of higher education. This is partly because doubt is research's foremost assistant, and partly because what is going on in the universities probably wasn't all that exciting in the first place. Inside, capable people may be found—capable in their own fields. But there are other fields and activities. Perhaps even more is required of the person who grows tomatoes or builds a house? Or perhaps such activities produce an even greater return on the investment? The "normalization" of the highest levels of education breeds what we could call "neopopulism"—an important brake on the tendency toward the professionalization of society (cf. Torgersen 1971). In addition, the security of material abundance—allowing for social experiments—is eroding the foundation of the class structure. The same can be said for the trends in youth culture that are making new ways of life seem more respectable. A lack of clarity rises like a phoenix out of these ruptures, weakening the intimate connection between high levels of education and high social status.

In line with this, academic salaries are decreasing. This is by all means beneficial for the education system. We will never be completely rid of the problems described in this book, however, as long as salaries are based on education levels. Schools will attract opportunists looking for monetary gain rather than for teaching. There is no need to take a stand on whether trying to get rich is a legitimate goal. But it is certainly harmful to the education system when this goal is pursued through the institutions whose main function is to confer a status that in turn legitimizes a higher salary. In such cases, it becomes impossible to alleviate the pressure on the education system. In such cases, we end up constructing a shortage of space at all levels of education and thereby centrifuges within the public school.

It is becoming increasingly unreasonable to claim that the poor academic deserves material circumstances that are slightly better than those of most people, allegedly so as to provide the conditions necessary to enable them to carry out their lofty and difficult errand. When most people do well with less, it should be evident that the academic can function with less as well. It is utter nonsense that secondary school teachers should earn more than other teachers—surpassed in absurdity only by the model that allows teachers employed at the tertiary level (university professors most of all) to earn more than teachers in secondary schools. A decent school system cannot be established before a comprehensive educational maintenance allowance is instated, followed by a fixed salary for the entire education sector, possibly with additional compensation for parents with children, certain age groups, or certain remote districts. In addition, it seems about time to finally put into motion mechanisms that can control admission to the few professions over which society has some influence—mechanisms beyond that of the formal education system. There is a long waiting list for students wishing to study medicine and odontology. We should therefore reduce the salary of these overly popular fields of study in order to shorten the waiting list. The most zealous will presumably stay. It is hard to take seriously those who see an unsolvable problem in the fact that many candidates seek admission to studies offering the most enticing financial rewards.[5]

A new situation will arise when moderately paid teachers in schools and universities are freed from the task of certifying people for a higher pay grade (at least in terms of the government's regulated salary levels). At the higher and highest levels of education—in the sense of institutions dealing with the most complicated or comprehensive fields of knowledge—teachers will meet students who are above all there to learn. At the primary and lower secondary school levels, teachers will be able to take care of not only the need to learn but also the need for a place to be.

The pressure described in first part of this section will foster a development of this nature. It will not happen overnight—especially not in the case of upper secondary schools, as they are staffed with highly specialized individuals holding traditionally high statuses and no immediately apparent alternatives. The fight for admission to the best upper secondary schools will continue in other parts of Norway, even if universities open up little by little for students without upper secondary school diplomas (a fully open university will probably never come to pass without struggles of considerable magnitude). The fight will also continue even if everyone is granted the right to attend upper secondary school—hereby forcing these schools to change simply because they are no longer recruiting the students they want the most. Especially in districts with traditionally low levels of education, the educational pyramid will take more time to become heavy at the top—the upper secondary school diploma will endure as a confirmation of the status an individual has been born to achieve. If the primary and lower secondary schools refuse to distinguish "the best" from the rest in leaving certificates, upper secondary schools could perform this assessment at the beginning of the first term through admission tests. It would be illusory to believe that the stratifying function of the education system will disappear—the prospects of this coming to pass are relegated to the very, very distant future. But this, of course, is a political question. Can we tolerate such a system? Let us, in any case, try to minimize its impact.

One could try to hinder direct transitions between educational levels. How about a few years of work first? This would perhaps create new problems—and these will be addressed below. And if secondary schools remained cramped, why not come up with different admission criteria? A raffle would certainly work better—and do less harm to the losers of the established system—than both compulsory lesson plans and tests. And it would also—to the extent that children from upper- and middle-class families lost out—lead to a rapid expansion of the capacity of upper secondary schools. Naturally, such schemes would generate new problems. These will remain unsolved for now. We must move on to another important matter. It will annoy those in power—but perhaps entice those who are not.

## A MIRROR FOR SCHOOLS

There are many reasons why schools have turned out the way they have. These reasons make implementing change appear hopeless. What I have proposed will probably be rejected as utopian and irrelevant by many. Let me try to shake up the latter assumption a little by holding up a mirror borrowed from the toolbox of research in criminology. It is an unusual vantage point for looking at the school as a system (but normal when looking at students). We are accustomed to comparing the most ordinary educational institutions to each other—primary schools, secondary schools, and universities. But humor me by permitting me to make an analogy comparing the lower secondary schools to prisons.

Let us first try to perceive these institutions through the eyes of the most estranged students: the dropouts, those with hairy chins or puffed-out chests, those with great vigor and on average higher activity levels than they will ever experience again, and those with an intense need to behave like fully grown adults. I would dare say that such students' experience of their own situation quite often resembles that of a prisoner's. They find themselves within an authoritarian system from which they cannot escape. They are compelled by law to stay. If they skip school, they can be fetched by those in power and be transferred to another institution. Parents can be punished if their children do not show up. In this system, students are on the lowest rung of the ladder, while everyone else, absolutely everyone else, has the right to give them orders they must obey. Those in power coordinate their actions and information. What is known by one is usually made available to and known by everyone in the system. This information will also be communicated to others in power—parents or administrative authorities, who then provide additional information in return. Since these young people have no expectations of staying in school, much of the planned schoolwork will seem meaningless. Consequently, their schoolwork frequently obtains the *quality of slave labor*—like moving stones from one end of the yard to the other and then back again. Modern prison facilities have at least tried to legitimize these structures by offering actual work, some even including paid positions. Schoolwork remains unpaid. Nonetheless, the work of students is meticulously checked by school authorities, and the results of these checks are made public and available to everyone, including the other students. It is hard work. Unlike slave labor, both the relative and more general sense of a student's failure in school is degrading, also in the eyes of their fellow prisoners.

⌐ within this external framework, the internal life of ⌐he school obtains several characteristics in common with the life we know from prison research. Some students join forces to form a common front against the teachers, widening the distance between them: norms *against* cooperation are created. These norms are directed in part at the teachers and in part toward fellow students who display weakness—in other words, a willingness to cooperate with the oppressors. There are quite obvious reasons behind these acts of dissent. They symbolize what side the student is on in the everlasting battle against persons in positions of authority. They generate excitement, break up the monotony of daily life, and contribute, at least to some degree, to creating a feeling of ownership—a feeling of still being free.

Interesting similarities appear between lower secondary schools and correctional facilities in a number of areas: to a large extent, neither of these institutions have any real possibility of sanctioning their clientele. At first glance, this may seem like a paradox: the prison, surrounded by walls, filled with authorities trained to do the job, equipped with keys and handcuffs, and granted permission by society, with the force of the police and military up their sleeves—how can the prison staff be without any possibility for sanctions? As for the schools, did I not just say that *everyone* has power over students, and that those in this position of coordinated power have at their disposal the most draconian control mechanisms to ensure that each student completes the assigned schoolwork? Yes, but nevertheless—or perhaps for precisely this reason, the prisoner has already hit bottom and quite simply cannot descend any further. They have already been deprived of everything a human being can be deprived of. If decency prevents us from using a whip or other forms of torture, starvation or complete isolation for more than limited periods of time, then there is nothing more to take from them. Then we are truly powerless. And the prisoner is free. We are also powerless in relation to the *student* who has had enough, doesn't want to continue studying, and has messed up for one reason or another. I would expect most prison wardens to nod in recognition when hearing about the apparent "disciplinary problems'" of many schools. The teacher is not so lucky. Their job was not presented as a job of internment. They were not trained to carry out their office. And they are even more restricted in their possibilities for exercising the requisite power. They are not allowed to employ any form of physical punishment. And they are charged with the responsibility of guarding a clientele who are free to complain to people outside the system every single day.

Yet at the same time, the teacher shares an important hurdle with the prison warden since *they cannot punish by means of exclusion*. The student, on the other hand, has plenty of ways to punish the teacher by staying away from school. If students skip school, this *may* lead to someone questioning the teacher's competence. If enough students stay away, this also raises doubts about the unquestioned justification of schooling. Truants do not only create problems for themselves. They shed a harsh light on the schools' function as a system of coercion and thereby fundamentally subvert the key mechanism of power employed by almost all other social systems: "If you don't want to follow the rules, get out of here."

In such situations, schools and teachers often resort to using many of the control mechanisms also used by prisons and prison wardens. They refrain from speaking about rights as much as possible when granting the wishes of a student. Rather, these wishes are portrayed as privileges or extraordinary benefits, which can be applied punitively, through withdrawal. Rights are taken for granted; privileges are instruments of control. The traditional prisons had cultivated this practice to perfection. Prisoners were divided into different classes—yes exactly, classes—and then each inmate would be granted an increasing number of privileges as they ascended through the ranks. Breaking the rules led to a downgrade in rank and withdrawal of privileges. This system was abandoned as the development of society made the preposterousness of claiming that not all prisoners deserved to begin in the best class patently evident. There were no longer any privileges. There were rights.

Prisons are, of course, not entirely without options. A difficult and/or dangerous prisoner can be transferred to a more secure prison, closed unit, or solitary confinement. Schools have similar options. They can send students to observation classes for difficult students, or reform school or other schools designed for troublemakers. Compared to the prisons, schools appear to offer more options for internal variation and less external control. Some of these schemes may even be seen as a good thing for some students. At the same time, however, reservations about the use of institutional transfers as an exercise of power will presumably be greater in schools than in prisons. This is due to the facts that the objective of detention in the school is covert and the ideological belief that all students should be able to function in an ordinary classroom environment is highly pervasive. It would feel like a failure for both the teacher and school to resort to removal. Once again—as in prison—it is probably easier to diagnose the renegade child and thereby displace responsibility onto the shoulders of other professions. Here as well as in more general attempts to curb smaller frictions within an individual prison or school, apparent parallels between the roles of prison doctors and school psychologists are found.

We are all subject to coercion, of course. The body coerces us, the twenty-four-hour day coerces us, the rhythms of the seasons impose their own demands, and time causes things to grow, mature, and decay. Most of us submit to these forces, or perhaps even feel a certain joy in succumbing or playing along with—and not against—the laws of nature. Socially constructed coercion—*when it is experienced as that*—is an entirely different story. I was recently leafing through the pages of some textbooks intended for ninth graders—one on health studies, another an English book, and the third a chemistry book. I can say without any reservations: exciting books, thoughtfully and elegantly composed, and a temptation for anyone—*anyone, that is, who chooses to become absorbed with them.* But as soon as they become mandatory reading, they are transformed from temptations into burdens—not for everyone, but a heavy one for some, and thereby highly contagious for many. There are also structures to be found within the inner life of schools that destroy what otherwise could have been a source of edifying joy— such as the joy of consistently studying the same subject for several weeks' time. Instead, by splitting up every school day into different subjects, students are systematically trained to work in a distracted manner, tossed from Roman emperors to music class to mathematics, then led through a brief stint of

physical education before arriving at German. Anyone wishing to demonstrate the manufactured coercion of this system
could hardly find a more telling example. This structure also
serves as an effective formula for the creation of an indifferent human being (cf. Carling 1966b; Hem 1971). Schools are,
to a certain extent, organized as subject-based institutions by
employing different teachers, each of whom have specialized
in a particular subject. On the one hand, such specialization
impedes many aspirations for a positive school experience.
On the other hand, the school day is organized in a way
that is contrary to the elementary principles of concentration. As such, the subjects themselves will not be taught
properly. This is, again, the result of the inner logic of the
school system, but at the same time a result that contributes to highlighting the similarities between schoolwork and
forced labor. Who can seriously recommend the merits of a
system that obliges the student to let go of one thought after
forty or forty-five minutes only to plunge into something
completely different, followed by a third topic, and then a
fourth. … Educational tricks are of little import when the
very framework, the timetable, is counterproductive.

Even in my most vindictive moments, I would not claim
that the analogy between lower secondary schools and prisons is completely fitting. But some things do fit, for some
students and teachers, in some situations. And regardless of
whether the analogy is fitting to a greater or lesser degree, I
find it important to call attention to these possibilities for
systematic resemblances. In so doing, I have simultaneously
described the antithesis to the preamble cited at the beginning of this book: this is no place to be if by "place" one
refers to a worthy place for human beings. If an institution

is built primarily for the purpose of storage, and defines students as its lowest and formally speaking most powerless participants, a prison is the obvious analogy. As such, I see no reason why educators should not familiarize themselves with the sociology of prisons rather than obscuring the similarities outlined above.

But that is not what we want. We do not want to convert schools into prisons. When I exaggerate the analogy to such an extreme, it is above all to reveal its dangerous proximity and inspire as many people as possible to work for the development of a school community with entirely different qualities than those of correctional facilities.

## A MIRROR FOR PARENTS

Naturally, it is not only the teachers and students who bear the brunt of this. The parents are also affected. When young people are made superfluous in our society, we simultaneously create a situation in which the possibility for control is greatly diminished for all age groups. Participation in the workforce implies the right to certain types of rewards, such as money, amenities, or respect. Exclusion from working life implies a general removal of these rewards. Parents and others are thereby also deprived of those power mechanisms that lie within *reducing rewards in response to significantly poor performance or other undesirable behavior*. Nothing can be taken back where nothing is given. Young people *as a group* are punished by this general exclusion from ordinary working life to the extent that there is nothing left to punish them for. It is not possible to punish the most disenfranchised even more through further exclusion.

But those who aspire to control the behavior of young people face other difficulties as well. In communities with scant resources, deviants will quickly experience the consequences of dissent: exclusion from the community, and possibly hunger, dire necessity, or even ruin. In today's society, these basic sanctions are no longer an option—in part because our values dictate that it is wrong to starve maladjusted youths, but above all, it simply cannot be done. There are so many basic resources readily available that most—if allowed freedom of movement—would find a way to survive if they were willing to endure a low standard of living. And that is exactly what many of them are not only willing to do but also view as an ideal.

I find it remarkable that in spite of everything, society is functioning as well as it is, and people form connections with one another through emotion alone. The misconduct of adolescents is often the cause of public dismay—and that is probably because many of those in power actually do comprehend, or at least sense, how fragile the balance actually is. If the well-meaning society is unable to placate grievances, few punitive measures remain at its disposal as an alternative. The only remaining recourse is that of direct physical coercion: a beating or institution. Here, the situation of parents resembles that of prison guards. To inflict physical punishment runs counter to important values. Oddly enough, the physical punishment of adolescents is experienced as even more improper than infliction of the same on young children. And it is considered an admission of failure to seek help from other authorities. In an elegant analysis, Gresham Sykes (1958) shows how prison guards, with all the power in the world behind them, rarely exercise this power even when they have to—such as chastising the prisoner, shoving them, or worst of all, calling for help—because to do so implies they are unskilled in their vocation. Instead, they try to achieve cooperation through the use of all manner of compromises and thereby are to a large degree controlled by their prisoners. Parents are in a somewhat similar situation, chiefly because children and especially young people possess a key resource within the situation to which we have brought both ourselves and them: they can refuse to participate. The student can escape—they can withdraw or seek out the company of peers. Society's formerly integrated punishments for withdrawing from the workforce have ceased to be effective; the students are already excluded. And they do not starve to death. Viewed from this perspective, the symbolic presence of the Palace Park in Oslo or the city of Copenhagen are probably more important for youths who do *not* hang out in the Palace Park and do not travel to Copenhagen than for those who actually do. *The possibility* of leaving is power. It is a onetime weapon, functioning like the threat of divorce in a marriage. Like a nuclear weapon, it is so powerful that it is more effective when it is not used. But the mere possibility has an effect. In the back of their minds, both parties know that the young person can commit acts that would bring the authorities to the very brink of desperation. The more horrifying the descriptions of the deserted backyards occupied by rebellious youths in Copenhagen for the purpose of carrying out different projects, the greater the potential threat afforded to ordinary adolescents. Those who leave give power to those who stay.

## A PLACE TO BE

We will now leave behind the prisons and the possibility of a large-scale adolescent withdrawal from society behind us, and take another look at the Standing Committee on Education and Church Affairs' (Recommendation to the Odelsting XLV, 1968–1969, 9) important words about the act it created concerning primary and lower secondary education:

> We must therefore, to a much greater extent, begin to view our schools as social communities. Schools can and must do more than prepare and qualify students for the life ahead of them. Schools *are in their own right* an essential part of life. Education has become—and will be even more so—an increasingly integral part of what it means to be a human being. Schools must therefore have an *intrinsic value*. Children and young people should be able to find joy in their existence while attending school. It will hence become a key responsibility for schools to promote well-being and happiness.

If it is the case that we have set up society in such a way that there is no use for people in that society until they reach a certain age—and have chosen instead to gather them in institutions we have called schools—we should then direct our efforts toward converting these institutions into a type of miniature society where life can be lived to the fullest and in the most ordinary form as a matter of course. We do happen to know quite a bit about what such a life would entail insofar as we agree that it should have as few qualities as possible in common with prisons. The antithesis to the prison is an open society, where all parties participate because they feel like it, find something valuable to take home with them, and/or the time spent together in and of itself yields significant benefits. In our context, this means that the public school must first and foremost be a place to be, before it is a place to learn.

When sociologists speak of "society," they are often referring to social systems that are self-sufficient, self-governing, and to a large extent independent of others. Norway is a society, but the Norwegian State Railways is not. Yet Norway may be less of a society in some periods and more so in others. Isolated villages may be distinct societies, but with the arrival of better roads this characteristic tends to disappear.

Questions concerning the organization of social life are probably of less importance in a school for adults aspiring to become airline pilots. Here the purpose of going to school is apparent: to acquire knowledge. It is evident for all involved parties that a great deal of this knowledge is necessary, so it is reassuring when the acquired level of knowledge is tested before students leave the school. Their education has an immediate relevance to their future occupation.

The opposite is the case for many students in lower secondary school. And the qualities of the social system as a community become correspondingly important. This pertains to individuals who have been deprived of meaningful tasks in their daily lives due to technological advancements and do not necessarily obtain qualifications for any type of employment through the course of their schooling. In such schools, the life of the society *is* the actual content. The challenge facing the school must therefore be to offer the option of participation—and hereby opportunities to find meaning—within a social system in which ordinary life is represented to the greatest possible extent. That is, precisely, a society. A society has at least *five* characteristics, which should also characterize such a school-society.

1. They should, like all societies, have a certain degree of *autonomy*. This is what is achieved by cutting down on external administration, a compulsory curriculum, and most of the tests. I have said enough about this above.

2. Another characteristic is *self-sufficiency*. In relation to schools, this could be achieved by granting schools full control over their own buildings and equipment, including their immediate surroundings. In the current society, we struggle to provide children with meaningful tasks—tasks that they can master—and where the importance of such mastery is self-evident. In the current situation, we do our utmost *within* the school *to deny* children and young people the possibility of undertaking such meaningful tasks. To begin with the most elementary ones, Why in the world is the cleaning of the school premises not left to the users of the school? Why is the repainting of classrooms not a task for the school? Outside there are lawns, maybe even parks. Perhaps there is a schoolyard in need of gravel or asphalt, light bulbs to be changed, wastepaper to be disposed of, mail to be distributed, and bulletin boards to be decorated. Why not leave all this to the actual members of the school-society?

I know the answers:

A. We do not have time to take care of such matters due to the scheduled curriculum and tests.

B. It will be both expensive and inefficient. I speak from experience. Some time ago, I wrote a short article containing some of my thoughts that led Per Aavatsmark to propose the following during the budgetary negotiations in Oslo in 1968: "In collaboration with the education authorities, the administration is urged to shed light on the question of whether schools should be in charge of their gardens, preferably in a school gardening class." The chief technical officer established a committee that responded, "The tasks vary greatly and change with the seasons. A large number of the tasks clearly call for skilled workers. ... [U]p to now this work has been led and for the most part carried out by skilled and experienced gardeners. To the greatest extent possible, they use gardening machinery." The commission deemed it inadvisable, and the chief technical officer added, "It may be even more expensive to implement the proposed solution. Teachers must receive pay for their work in supervising the students. Moreover, procuring machinery and tools for all schools would generate high costs." And the municipal financial officer agreed with the chief education officer on advising against such madness.

C. Moreover, it is not certain that the job would be done properly. The schools would not be as clean, neat, and shiny as they are today.

These responses are suitable for our purposes in that they illustrate key differences in the visions of what a school is or should be. If the school is considered an important place to be, it essentially goes without saying that the school itself should be responsible for the upkeep of the school building and determining the appropriate standards for that upkeep. This task, in and of itself, of arriving at decisions about how people want their school to be, is a matter of great importance for any school-society. How much energy should be devoted to cleaning, and how much money should be spent on paint? Who should decide, and how will agreements be reached? More than anything, these decisions will breed precisely the kind of tasks most educators claim to be looking for, whereby people who are good at organizing, can organize; people who are good at cleaning, can clean; those who are happy painters, can paint; and those who are strong in body can carry things while those who are not can make a marvelous contribution by baking bread for those doing the carrying. Of all the unimaginative initiatives in the history of curriculum-bound schooling, the most extreme example must be the decision to have ready-made food brought in to provide a nourishing breakfast, or even worse, where both produce and skilled housewives are brought in, thereby depriving the school kitchen of its completely natural service within the school-society: to prepare wholesome food when food is needed (and preferably a bit more often).[6] I can just envision the administrators sharpening their pencils as they prepare to write a memo specifying the particular foods that must be prepared. So let me quickly add, the type, substance, schedule, and expenses should, of course, also be determined by the school-society. If people want to serve beefsteak, so be it. Maybe the cost of that beefsteak will mean that they won't be able to afford their next school trip—but that is also their business.

This is a fundamental point for creating a thriving school-society. But passing half measures will yield the most lamentable results. Many a school administrator would claim that they really *have tried* to offer their students meaningful service tasks in relation to the school. They have encouraged the students to wash, paint, and garden. And the students can't be bothered. Just as they can't be bothered to pick up trash, or keep the school's common areas nice and tidy.

This raises the question of whether the school is society's school, the teachers' school, or really the *school-society's* school. Who determines whether its buildings need to be cleaned or painted, and how to spend any available savings? Those in power would like to experiment with changes that *first* impose duties on their subjects, and *thereafter*—if all goes well over a long period of time—gradually and tentatively introduce rights. Should the entire scheme prove untenable, the second part of the experiment will be dropped. But duties and rights must come hand in hand if the school is to work as envisioned.

No society can exist solely on the basis of the mutually provided services of its members. External resources must also flow into the school-society. In our context, this primarily implies that the school must actively find tasks to carry out both inside *and* outside the school. It probably won't have to look very far. Is it not grotesque that nursing homes and schools, located across the street from each other, toil desperately away in isolation in their mutual and separate endeavors to solve opposite problems? Nursing homes are in need of nursing staff, and schools are in need of meaningful tasks for their students. Why shouldn't class 8A be assigned full responsibility for a large part of the manual work required in the nursing home throughout the year? Why shouldn't class 8B be responsible for doing the daily grocery shopping for the district's elderly residents who are living alone or stopping by on a regular basis to make sure everything is all right? Why do we count on engineers to invent emergency alarm systems for the elderly who live alone when there is an abundance of young people in our society whom we have absolutely no idea what to do with, beyond keeping them in a school to learn something deemed important by the established educational conventions? Such service tasks require organization and coordination; they can be expanded, spill over into other activities, and even become a source of income for the school. Other schools will find other opportunities. They will most likely always operate on the margins—a bit on the outskirts—of ordinary working life in society. But this is where newcomers have always begun.

If only somebody would see the wisdom of these ideas. But then they would also have to have the strength to resist the temptation to impose a system. Memos and standardized schemes designed for universal use, or worse yet, an office or staff employed to perform this task—this would be enough to squelch anything of significance within the school-society. There is a widespread misconception—existing in sweet harmony with the special interests of many people—that social systems yield the best results when they are supplied with abundant material resources. Once again, however, the application of common sense reveals that the opposite will tend to be the case—as is exemplified in schools and universities. I have said enough about school administration, and I will only add that my points are valid for universities as well: an understaffed administration will make it self-evident that students and teachers must deal with the most pressing issues together. In this way the fight over resources is avoided.

This is especially important in the school-society. Here, a shortage of staff implies that everyone must be put to use— even the least capable of students must not simply be tolerated but instead be encouraged to pitch in. In such cases, everybody wins. The smaller schools must send everyone out onto the field when their team is playing—otherwise their efforts will come to naught. The larger schools have the luxury of using their best players and excluding the others. Whether small schools are better than large at imparting knowledge to their students remains unclear. Yet they are most certainly better at creating the conditions to ensure a life of participation.[7] It is, in this light, clearly not helpful to supply the school-society with all kinds of external resources and provide it with all manner of support so only those who are truly qualified have an opportunity to put their talents to use. Insofar as we conceive of the school as a society, it must to a large degree manage itself in order for its members to manage themselves. The administrator's task—if they have not already been phased out—must be to look away, bite their tongue, keep their mouth shut, let the school manage on its own, and if worse comes to worse, offer to help put out the severest of fires. Or put differently, the administrator should act in relation to the particular school as reasonable parents do with their children—walk beside them, ready to provide support, and only intervene when absolutely necessary.

3. *Socialization.* Every society must eventually accept new recruits and ensure that they fit in—that they are welcomed as fellow members of society. Once more, it is helpful to think of the school as a type of miniature society. And once more, this is a worthy task for those who have personally lived in that society for weeks, months, or years. A central task of this school-society should be that older students function as teachers for newcomers. Educationists have a technical term for this—"peer mentoring"—and it fell into disrepute, perhaps rightly, in the middle of

the last century. At the time, it was a makeshift solution designed to compensate for the shortage of teachers, and drill students in the most elementary levels of reading, writing, and calculus. But today, we face a luxury problem. Our predominant challenge is how to help people learn to live with one another.

4. Some students will mess around, though. They will refuse to play by the rules of the school-society. An infinite number of hours will be spent on determining what these rules are as well as what constitutes their violation, why such breaches happen, and their potential consequences. This theme can be summarized as *deviance and social control*, the core challenges of which constitute utter nightmares for principals and head teachers. In many aspects, the roles of the police officer and head teacher are quite similar, with the important difference being that the police officer enjoys a nobler reputation for snatching up worthier villains. If we hope to create a thriving school-society, these duties must be taken out of the hands of the authorities and placed in the hands of the school-society. I do not imagine that there are many authorities who take pleasure in these tasks, but nonetheless there are real difficulties and risks associated with handing them over to the actual members of the school-societies. Abuses of power may occur. In addition, every educator will know that students can behave even more harshly toward their peers—often to the point of barbaric cruelty—than the most apathetic of teachers. First, however, a school-society is certainly not an authoritarian framework, and second, it is not my intention to abolish the teachers but rather to employ them differently. More on this later.[8]

5. It would be a paltry society if we were to stop here. Much like our current situation, it would be a society where rituals are few and dull, where high culture is extremely high, reserved only for connoisseurs, where legends and myths are written in books, and hash smokers have a monopoly on transcendent experiences. Something has been lost that must be secured by the school-society. The same holds true for *art and religion*, which will be addressed in a bit.[9]

*"And who should decide?"*

The overall bent of my proposals is probably clear about now. The school-society should decide on who should decide. Several problems arise from this answer. The most apparent problem probably pertains to the boundaries of the society: Who has the right to influence and decide? As I see it, the more schools are forced to uphold their functions of storage and stratification, the more we should push back, and the more reasonable it becomes to leave it up to the students and teachers to make as many of the decisions as possible on their own. Parents, in this sense, become adversaries of the school-society, looking for a place to store their children as well as certify them for the highest-possible social position. They become a pressure group advocating for more subjects, more tests, more lesson planning, and less life. It is easy to understand why teachers often try to protect themselves— and their students—from parents who zealously try to make schools increase whatever they already have too much of in the first place. In this situation, it makes sense to ensure that parents have little say about the particularities of each school. But the more schools become places for authentic engagement with important elements of the surrounding world, the more this surrounding world will be invited to engage. This means first and foremost the parents, but also locally elected school boards. When there is a substantial influx of these outside resources, there is every reason to expect that the older children, whom this is about, will be able to understand this. The interests of the children and parents will hereby converge. Parents will, in effect, *be* represented in the school-society. And then the question concerning decision making will become to a large extent immaterial.

*"And the teachers?"*

The teachers will become—now as before—the most important partners in the school-society. But they will be partners—not commanders. They will become adult coworkers, occupied with the task of integrating the most valuable elements from the surrounding society into the life of the school-society. They will be given opportunities to impart models for adult life through a much wider range of activities than were previously made available. They will assert their positions as teachers through their actions within the school-society, as sources of inspiration, or supervisors or sages—depending on whatever qualities they may possess. A few teachers without these qualities would serve as the school-society's deviants, highlighting the value of the school-society's norms precisely through their noncompliance. They would be assigned simpler chores on the margins of the system, and some would have to face the sanctions determined by the school-society, either in the form of treatment or punishment.

The children would not terrorize one another. If there is one certainty about most children, it is their wish to grow out of such habits. Adults unburdened by family ties to children attending the school will always have extraordinary opportunities for influencing them. In the case of those of today's youths who aspire to become adults in a manner that differs from our foolish approach, perhaps they are right to question and should have the power to vote down the teacher. But I do not think this will lead to problems in the way of low standards, chaos, or extravagance. They would on average probably be young people who are even stricter, more serious, more determined, and more demanding of themselves and others than is perhaps beneficial for society. The youth demonstrations that now and then arise (even in Norway) indicate something important about young people, but are not representative of the vast majority.

## A PLACE TO LEARN

In becoming a place to be, the school-society also becomes a place to learn. Here, I defend a sort of working-school principle. If we wish for our students to become competent and independent people, who are able to maintain a home and function in society, they must learn this through life and participation, not by going through the motions. It is here that the Norwegian Parliament's imperative to "endeavor to facilitate constructive modes of cooperation" should be taken into serious consideration. If students are to learn about and become familiar with the life of society, they should live a life in society. There can be no other way.

But proper participation requires a large number of things: developing the rules for the school-society requires reading and writing skills. The rules must be read and written, and perhaps even typed up. Campaign speeches for school elections must be written; arguments must be worked out in detail and based on information. Budgets must be created, and salaries must be calculated along with questions of, How much should we charge for the cinnamon buns? Most people will find doing such calculations enjoyable if they are keeping track of things that they really need. There is no need to detail the specific configurations of this work. There is an abundance of life and activities to work on both inside and outside our schools.

For all my talk about schools as places to be, we must not forget another easily overlooked and perhaps even more important fact: humans are not sustained solely by community. Once again, there is cause to consider schools in relation to the laws of historical change. For example, the schools in Norway were historically tied to the word of God. Bishops and pastors controlled the teacher, and did so with an iron fist. A large part of the battle for better schools in Norway has been a battle against the dominant position of Christianity studies. The growth in school administrations and compulsory lesson plans can be explained in a similar fashion. If the local community were granted too much decision-making latitude, too much time would be spent singing hymns in school. There are still too many hymns being sung, but perhaps this is now done in a more perfunctory way. The law dictates that schools provide students with a Christian upbringing, but this is—because of the way Norwegian society has developed—mostly carried out by non-Christian people. The result is probably even worse than not having such courses. The knowledge of Christianity is taught in accordance with the law and, in effect, becomes a history class. But it is a rather improbable history, at odds with everything else that is taught. In all other subjects, another world is taught—a world completely untouched, and unaffected by religious issues and events, since these are presumed covered in the course on Christianity.[10]

This is perhaps all well and good, given how the school is set up today. Young people are left to their own devices in their efforts to make sense of and gain perspective in their lives. But in the *school-society*, these themes must not be left in the shadows: they must be included, not as subjects of learning, but in the manner of life experience. Once again, we arrive at the need for *complete school-societies*, offering a life of rituals and possibilities for artistic development or to experience art.

It is important that the sad fate of Christianity studies in schools should not become a pattern. At the same time, it is crucial that we acknowledge the need for new forms of spirituality. Fredrik Barth (1961) describes how his search for religious experience led him to wander with a Persian nomadic people. He did not discover their religious practices until after he finished his book—his portrait can be found, in any case, in the book's appendix. Here, he describes how wandering itself *is* the religion of these people, how it is to depart, pack up, and set out on their journey to a distant and promised land, moving ever more quickly as they approach their destination, leaving before daybreak, making camp in the evening, and then finally the journey's climax: they arrive, they have reached the place where they will live until the change of the season, at which point they will do it all over again in the opposite direction. Tarjei Vesaas (1934) depicts something similar in *The Great Cycle*. To a large degree, it is probably the same thing that Norwegian peasants have experienced and are experiencing, the absence of which causes city dwellers to yearn and search clumsily for *something else*.

Again, we see this yearning for something else most clearly in the more recent generations that have only experienced the current society. We see its importance in the consumption of hash as well as other and more dangerous drugs. We see it in pilgrimages toward the mysticisms of the East. We see it in the many music festivals. And we see it in small gatherings. The historian Theodore Roszak (1969, 194) provides a description that applies to many of these cases:

> The tribalized young gather in gay costume on a high hill in the public park to salute the midsummer sun in its rising and setting. They dance, they sing, they make love as each feels moved, without order or plan. Perhaps the folklore of the affairs is pathetically ersatz at this point—but is the intention so foolish after all? There is the chance to express passion, to shout and stamp, to caress and play communally. All have equal access to the event; no one is misled or manipulated. Neither kingdom, nor power, nor glory is desperately at stake. Maybe, in the course of things, some ever discover in the commonplace sun and the ordinary advent of summer the inexpressible grandeur that is really there and which makes those who find it more authentically human.

Humans are not good animals. Even when they are well off and well fed, they are afflicted with restlessness and longing—states that are by all means unworthy of a technocracy. But if the schools we seek to create are to live and breathe, they must spring from and exist for these longings.

Once again, we must recognize that we, along with our schools, are works in progress. The conventional church no longer holds the power it once did. We do not need to worry about becoming entangled in its web. And even if we were to become entangled, it would probably be because the church did have something to offer after all, so it would be fine. Today, our lives have been stripped of the possibility for rituals. But again, material suffering has become so remote for us that we have the capacity to long for something more and enable others do so as well. The ninth graders brave enough to spend the entire school year staging an adaptation of Finn Carling's (1966a) play about his zoological garden—besides, of course, baking bread, taking care of the community's elderly, and participating frenetically in the political life of their school—probably did the most important and meaningful thing they could have done that year. They read the play, became absorbed with its plot, built the stage sets, hated each other's differing interpretations, and experienced themselves and one another in the characters as well as in relation to the play as a whole. And when it was all over, they had learned something that was worth knowing.

## A USELESS SCHOOL?

Some will hold that this would be worse than if the school were to be closed. Schools as school-societies would create useless people. But the division of subjects, vast differences in status within the school system, hectic wandering from one subject to another, external administration, and students divested of responsibility—all this contributes to the creation of the indifferent human being. Overall this indifference, admittedly, is in accordance with the needs of society. It is *exactly* such people that society needs for the activities carried out on the assembly line or in the office, for all kinds of services. Society has no need for critical and dedicated people; everything would grind to a halt if society had too many of them. Maybe there is in fact no grand scheme behind the current system, no wish or intention to indoctrinate students in specific ways. Maybe the organization of the school arrived at its current form due to other—internal—reasons. Yet it was permitted to acquire this form because it somehow *fit*—and not just in terms of the demands for storage and stratification but also with respect to the type of human being created. Another type of school would not supply society with the type of citizens it needs. It would be doomed to failure.

I have already admitted that the chances of creating another type of school are minimal. This is, first and foremost, due to the requirements currently addressed by the schools. In important areas, a different type of school would demand or prompt other solutions—that is, a different society. Here too the chances are miniscule, chiefly due to the inner organization of schools. Differences in status would have to be equalized, and this would be a painful process. Many conflict-reducing mechanisms would be removed. The subjects that control our schools share the characteristic of being largely *harmless*—or at least that is how they are presented in schools. Subject specialists get along well as long as they experience each other and themselves as subject specialists. The physics teacher talks about physics, the Norwegian teacher talks about Norwegian, and then they talk among themselves about something else entirely during recess. They each have their own kingdom, and the borders are secured by the weekly schedule. The only real conflict that could possibly arise would be if an especially zealous teacher assigned overly ambitious amounts of homework, calling unreasonable amounts of attention to *their* subject. With the exception of this scenario, everyone proceeds in an atmosphere of peace and tolerance. Another teacher's subject is another teacher's property; there is little reason to interfere. There is also no reason to disagree about students—in part because the teachers are a bit fed up with them, and in part because such disagreements risk exposing a teacher's difficulties with them in front their peers. Ingrid Eide (1962) identified this as an important aspect when attempting to explain the remarkable tendency among teachers to avoid conversations about students and disciplinary problems.

A different type of school would eliminate all possibilities for finding refuge in the seemingly neutral subjects. Every single day, disagreements regarding views of life that are bound to exist in both the teachers' staff room and all other rooms where people meet would be mercilessly forced out of the shadows. Subject specialists would be obliged to step aside to make room for whole human beings. Harrowing divides would appear, and conflicts would erupt. There would no longer be a divide separating teachers from students. Instead, it would appear internally among the teachers, on the one hand, and internally among the students, on the other. The school would live an arduous life.

The chances of creating a different kind of school are minimal. But how minimal?

Pretty minimal. But a number of circumstances give cause for hope.

While life in this school might be arduous, it would also be rich. The current organization of schools is neither without its costs. The teacher's life is lonely; the breach between the teacher and students comes at a price. The subjects may provide a buffer, but they also supply a barrier. A different type of school would *offer* its members a great many things— including possibilities for developing a community based on an outlook on life. Important forces in our society may also make such a shift an urgent necessity. Uselessness is constantly on the rise. The storage function of schools has become so self-evident that the need for a different school appears increasingly justified. We cannot simply proceed as usual. This will soon be clear for the majority.

An additional hope lies in the growth of the technocracy. Irrespective of the ownership of the means of production, the number of manual tasks to be done is on the decline. This will increase surplus and uselessness—but it will help shift the attention to other people and away from things too. Our fellow human beings will be all that remains for us to work on. I do not hope, however, that the school I am proposing will educate its students in the reworking of human beings. But I do hope that it will educate students in how to *be together with other people* and thereby will begin to be more acceptable. The spontaneous dissolution of the education society also instills hope. Many with knowledge become many who doubt the value of knowledge. The emperor's new clothes become more and more threadbare.

And finally, the growth of the counterculture of youths. The students attending lower secondary school are far from empty rooms. They are young individuals with strong opinions and values that have no place whatsoever in the current school, but do have a place front and center in the school I have sought to promote. What a wonderful group of Native American students they might have been had we dared to let them assume the responsibility for creating a school where they could realize themselves and their values.

The school would not be a playground. It would not be a place for kind, cheerfully ruminating intellectuals. Not only that, at least. It would be a critical school and a space for conflict, not just harmony. This is where the protests commence. Some will be quick to say that it is impossible. Society could never tolerate such a school. I have doubts about such a critique. The word "society" denotes wholeness. Who—which person, or at least, which function—would endeavor to shut down such a good place to be and learn? Besides, many of today's counterculturalists finished school a long time ago and would do everything they could to ensure that their children were spared experiencing the same type of education.

There can be no theoretical answer to the questions raised above. There can only be the attempt to create a different school.

# 6

# A DREAM OF A SCHOOL

We have almost reached the end. At this point, some readers will look for clarification or an overview—a summary of the book in its entirety. If so, they will be disappointed. Instead, they will find a chapter about a place I am familiar with that is located way out in the countryside.

Somewhere in Norway there is a small cluster of houses, constituting a village of sorts. Some sixty to seventy people live here—the members of seven large families. The word "family" is used here in a broader sense than is usual. Some are married and have children, and others are part of the family in the sense that they live under the same roof—the house is also theirs, they share their lives in sorrow and joy, and count on doing all this in the future. The village has a bit of industry and farming. The days are spent socializing, and the evenings are divided between amusements, games, and what we might daringly label intellectual activities—reading, listening, or perhaps putting on a play. There is a lot to be learned about the self in playing the part of someone else.

Newcomers at the dinner tables of this village are always confused. It has fallen on me to bring my students to this place on many occasions, so I know what I am talking about. We travel around together and study different forms of social life. They don't know ahead of time what they will encounter, as I have found it is better to discuss this afterward. In this particular place, we are scattered among the village's seven houses, each of which accommodate ten to twelve inhabitants in addition to their guests. A meal is prepared, and dinner is served. And all the while, those of us who are newcomers struggle to put this world into some kind of order, put people into categories, and try to figure out who is who.

We will partake in many dinners before we finally make sense of everyone—and by that time, categories will no longer be of interest. A little more than half the people at the table are individuals who officially are labeled persons with disabilities. Some have serious mental illnesses on top of this. But such disabilities are barely noticed here. They are *able* within the framework that has been created. A way of life has been established that allows them to interact with "normal" people and live in a "normal" way.

And then there is one more thing about this place worth mentioning: it is teeming with young people. Officially it is defined as a nursing home—in other words, a place that ordinarily fights a desperate losing battle to make its residents stay there of their own free will. But at Vidaråsen, which is the name of the place, the problem is exactly the opposite: there are so many young people who wish to live there that the ordinary resident must be protected from not feeling alienated in their own home. Last summer this amounted to between twenty and thirty young people in addition to the usual residents who came to stay, work, and live there.

Because of the abundance of impulses, the inevitable came to pass: the community began to organize itself, and there were activities all hours of the day and night. Then a school emerged, as if of its own accord. It emerged in the evenings, of course. The word "school" means leisure in Greek.[1]

From the perspective of an outsider, it appeared that something else was happening too. In our current type of society, the people of most critical importance to this story are born into an impoverished life, destined to become a burden and embarrassment. But in the village-society described here, they become key players in the creation of a new whole. Their unusual constitutions impose unique requirements on the external environment. In order to function as ordinary residents, they must live in a social system characterized by what I have termed "community-mindedness." And lo and behold: if we succeed in establishing communities that are beneficial for "special" people, these communities will also be so good for everyone else that the latter will line up in droves for the chance to join them. The "special" person functions best within a type of society that others find attractive too. Around him or her, the good society can grow.[2]

The good school could perhaps also be a model, an innovator. Its community-mindedness would be groundbreaking and engender new structures. This school beyond the present school would be located perhaps in the neighborhood where children and adults would meet in cooperation and leisure— that is, in school. It would be a place where we would share the work in the same manner as our time for leisure. It would be a society in which we would use our inordinate prosperity to reflect on how we want our lives to be, free from oppression, free to direct our society in relation to values that our schools had demonstrated were worthy of realization.

My dream of a school is a dream of a society that has learned so much from its schools that the very notion of school for children and young people is defunct, has become superfluous, has become a part of life itself. It is a mode of existence in which the community-minded nature of schools has permeated our local communities in such a way that these communities have opened up to life and will no longer need special schemes to store their children somewhere separate from the society of which they are a part. The need for learning and maintenance of our shared cultural heritage will remain. But it will be a form of learning that arises in response to the actual experiences and desires of those seeking it, not stipulated by mandates on reaching a certain age.

My dream of a school is a dream of a society providing exactly the same thing as a good school would do. This can be nothing but a good society.

# KEY AGENCIES AND CONCEPTS

---

**Avgørelsesorgan**: decision-making body

**Bestyrer**: administrator

**Ekspedisjonssjef**: office manager

**Fagfolk**: subject specialists

**Faglærer**: subject teachers

**Fagskole**: subject-based school

**Finansrådmann**: chief financial officer

**Folkeskole**: people's schools

**Folkeskoleloven**: Education Act

**Forsøgsrådet**: National Council for Innovations in Education

**Førstelærer**: head teacher

**Grunnskole**: primary school

**Gymnas**: upper secondary school

**Hovedlærer**: homeroom teacher

**Kirke- og Undervisningsdepartementet**: Ministry of Education and Church Affairs

**Kirke- og Undervisningskomiteen**: Standing Committee on Education and Church Affairs

**Klasseforstander**: form teacher

**Kommunestyre**: city council

**Kursplan**: lesson plan

**Lov om Grunnskolen**: Primary and Lower Secondary Education Act

**Mønsterplan**: Curriculum Guidelines for Compulsory Education in Norway

**Myndighedspersoner**: School authorities (when used in relation to schools)

**Normalinstruks**: standard regulations or guidelines

**Normalplan (for grunnskolen)**: national curriculum (for compulsory education)

**Normalplanutvalg**: National Curriculum Committee

**Overlærer**: head teacher

**Reglementsutvalg**: Regulatory Committee

**Samarbeidsutvalget**: liaison committee

**Samvirkekomité**: Standing Committee on Cooperative Affairs

**Skolebestyrer**: principal

**Skoledirektøren**: municipal education commissioner

**Skolefolk**: educationists

**Skoleinspektør**: school inspector

**Skoleledelsen**: school administration

**Skoleleder**: district commissioner

**Skole rådmann**: school councillor

**Skolesjefen**: chief municipal education officer

**Skolestyre:** same as **skolestyret** below, indefinite form

**Skolestyrer:** school principal

**Skolestyret:** board of education / school board

**Teknisk rådmann:** chief technical officer

**Timefordelingstabellen:** weekly schedule

**Ungdomskontoret i Oslo:** Oslo Youth Office

**Ungdomsskole:** lower secondary school

**Videregående skoler:** upper secondary school

# NOTES

## INTRODUCTION

1. Christie's doctorate dissertation was published in 1960. Nils Christie, *Unge norske lovovertredere [young Norwegian law offenders]* (Oslo, Oslo University Press, 1960).

2. Heido Mork Lomell and Vidar Halvorsen, "Nils Christie, 1928–2015," *Journal of Scandinavian Studies in Criminology and Crime Prevention* 16, no. 2 (2015): 144.

3. Nils Christie, "Conflicts as Property," *British Journal of Criminology* 17, no. 1 (1977): 2.

4. Christie, "Conflicts as Property," 1.

5. Christie, "Conflicts as Property," 8, 7.

6. Most notably, Ivan Illich's *Deschooling Society* (New York: Harper and Row, 1971).

7. During his time as secretary of education in Rio, Brazilian educator Freire's engagement of the local communities in designing the frameworks for the communities' schools (*escola cidadã*) provides a succinct example of how this notion can be enacted in practice. See Moacir Gadotti and Carlos Alberto Torres, "Paulo Freire: Education for Development," *Development and Change* 40, no. 6 (2009): 1255–1267.

8. Currently, the growing issue of surplus populations—referring to the surging number of (educated) adults looking for work—seems to indicate that the need for other and, in Christie's spirit, more communal modes of organizing the activation of society's members might be worth pursuing for older members of the population as well. See Nick Srnicek and Alex Williams, *Inventing the Future* (London: Verso, 2016).

9. For readers interested in further exploring these connections, we recommend Pierre Bourdieu and Jean-Claude Passeron's classic, *Reproduction in Education, Society, and Culture* (London: Sage, 1977).

10. The Camphill Schools are a global movement of nongovernmental schools serving children and youths with developmental disabilities. For more information on the Camphill movement—or to arrange a visit to one of its communities, as Judith Suissa describes in her essay—we encourage you to see www.camphillschool.org.

11. Paulo Freire, *Pedagogy of the Oppressed* (London: Continuum, 1970). See also Samuel Bowles and Herbert Gintis, *Schooling in Capitalist America* (New York: Basic Books, 1976).

12. "Interview with Betsy DeVos, the Reformer," *Philanthropy* (Spring 2013), https://www.philanthropyroundtable.org/philanthropy-magazine/article/spring-2013-interview-with-betsy-devos-the-reformer.

13. Jan Masschelein and Maarten Simons, *In Defense of the School: A Public Issue* (Leuven: Education, Culture and Society Publishers, 2014): 17.

14. Two classical works undergirding these positions, respectively, are US scholar Allan Bloom's *The Closing of the American Mind* (New York: Simon and Schuster, 1987), and French philosopher Jacques Rancière's *The Ignorant Schoolmaster: Five Lessons in Intellectual Emancipation* (Stanford, CA: Stanford University Press, 1991).

15. The widespread promotion of choice and performance measurement in global education policies are hallmark examples of how efficiency-oriented policies have tended to produce adverse results when looking at school segregation, social control, and academic improvement. For an overview of these policies and their effects in the contexts of the United States and United Kingdom, respectively, see Megan Erickson, *Class War* (London: Verso, 2015); Stephen Ball, *Global Education Inc.: New Policy Networks and the Neo-Liberal Imaginary* (London: Routledge, 2012).

16. Gert Biesta, *Good Education in an Age of Measurement: Ethics, Politics, Democracy* (London: Routledge, 2010), 2. See also Steen Nepper Larsen, "Blindness in Seeing: A Philosophical Critique of the Visible Learning Paradigm in Education," *Education Sciences* 9, no. 1 (2019): 1–12.

17. In their 2015 *Demain*, French filmmakers Mélanie Laurent and Cyril Dion document several ongoing projects where people are engaging in more sustainable relationships with their surroundings, inviting communities to engage more actively in the quality and development of various public services.

## CHAPTER 1

1. All references will be given in this form. A complete reference list can be found in the back of the book.

2. *Editors' note:* Although he doesn't specify as such, Christie is most likely referring to chapter 3.

3. *Editors' note:* In this passage, Christie conflates imagery from 19th century Dakota Territories with the conditions on the Lakota reservations in the 1960s. While both Sitting Bull (1831–1891) and Gerald One Feather (1938–2014) are associated with the Sioux Reservation in South Dakota, the vastly different political contexts surrounding their lives are somewhat obscured. Generally, when reading this passage, it is important to bear in mind that Christie is referring to the period in the Pine Ridge reservation as they are described by Wax and colleagues around the 1960's.

4. *Editors' note:* Christie uses the Norwegian word *Indianerne* (Indians) throughout the chapter in reference to the native population of the Pine Ridge reservation. In this text, the terms Native Americans or Sioux people will be used.

5. *Editors' note:* For readers interested in exploring the topic of cultural deprivation as it was discussed around the time of Christie's writing, Paul Willis's *Learning to Labor* (1977), Basil Bernstein's *Class, Codes and Control* (1971), and parts of Frantz Fanon's *The Wretched of the Earth* (1961) provide succinct analyses of the problematic relations between dominant cultures and upbringing in different contexts.

6. *Editors' note:* Anchored in the Butler Act of 1944 (also known as the 1944 Education Act), schools in England at the time of Hargreaves's study were structured around a highly meritocratic system. Generally, the system was based on sorting students into three variations of secondary schooling depending on their performance in the primary school leaving exam (known as "eleven-plus"), but districts such as Lumley has some degree of autonomy in designing their own system. In the introduction to the book cited by Christie, Hargreaves explains the Council in Lumley's policy for secondary schools, which provides a useful backdrop to the situation of Adrian and Clint:

> In Lumley School the pupils are streamed by ability and achievement. On entry, they are not specially assessed for allocation to streams. The Headmaster assigns boys to the five streams on the basis of their scores in the eleven-plus examination. Where two boys with the same eleven-plus score fall at a point of division between two streams, the boy with the more favourable Primary school report is assigned to the higher stream. The school is 'fed' by six main Primary schools, all of which are in the immediate vicinity of the school, and the new entrants are divided into five streams, A to E, the lowest (E) stream containing boys who are considered backward or retarded (Hargreaves 1967, 2).

7. *Editors' note:* Christie engages in wordplay here to highlight two points in the original text: the positions that the students find themselves in are both external (*ytre*) and extreme (*ytterliggående*).

## CHAPTER 2

1. There are, however, also important differences between the two. I have discussed some of these in relation to the field of criminology in Christie 1971.

2. Some of the content found in this chapter comes from three articles I have written on youths over the past three years. References to these articles can be found in the literature list (Christie 1968, 1969, 1970).

3. *Editors' note:* Christie's tale of the Norwegian family moving to town—and as a corollary, its negative implications for the children's usefulness—echoes a concern with *situated learning* formulated perhaps most clearly in the works of Dewey. In *The School and Society*, Dewey thus writes that "we cannot overlook the importance for educational purposes of the close and intimate acquaintance got with nature at first hand, with real things and materials, with the actual processes of their manipulation, and the knowledge of their social necessities and uses." J. Dewey, *The School and Society* (Chicago: University of Chicago Press, 2000), 8.

## CHAPTER 3

1. *Editors' note:* Cf. "A Place to Be" in chapter 5.

2. *Editors' note:* Dokka (1913–1999) was a Norwegian scholar at the University of Oslo from 1955–1980. Besides the doctoral dissertation that Christie references here, Dokka wrote several books, such as *Reforms in Norwegian Schools from 1950s to 1980* [Reformarbeid i norsk skole: 1950-årene—1980] (1981) and *250 Years of Schools* [En skole gjennom 250 år: den norske allmueskole, folkeskole, grunnskole 1739–1989] (1988).

3. *Editors' note:* Norwegian *rigsdaler* was a type of currency used in Norway between 1816 and 1878.

4. *Editors' notes:* Hovdhaugen (1908–1996) was a Norwegian politician, farmer, and public school teacher. He was the secretary general for the Farmer's Party in 1946–1949, and held positions in councils such as the Norwegian Language Council and Norwegian Broadcasting Council. He wrote eighteen books on a wide range of topics including immigration to the United States, cultural and local history, and issues relating to farming. He withdrew from his position on the Nobel committee after Henry Kissinger (b. 1923) and Lê Đức Thọ (1911–1990) were awarded

the Nobel Peace Prize in 1973. Also, until the system was abolished in 2009, the Norwegian Parliament consisted of two complementary units, the *Odelsting* and *Lagting*. The *Odelsting* was responsible for considering all bills before sending them on to the *Lagting*. In certain respects, the structure was similar to the current division of responsibility and powers between the House of Representatives and Senate in the US Congress.

5. *Editors' note:* Undheim (1905–1988) was a Norwegian politician and member of Parliament for the Center Party in 1961–1969. He was the principal of Rogaland High School in 1947–1972.

6. *Editors' note:* Dyring (1916–1975) was a Norwegian politician, member of the Norwegian resistance movement during World War II, and in charge of the Larvik area for the Norwegian Home Guard in 1948–1955. He was a member of Parliament for the Center Party in 1965–73.

7. *Editors' note:* Hovi (1905–1980) was a Norwegian politician, farmer, and member of Parliament in 1961–1973 for the Labor Party. He was a member of the Standing Committee on Education and Church Affairs (*Kirke- og undervisningskomitéen*) from 1965 to 1969.

8. *Editors' note:* Lindbekk (1933–2017) was a Norwegian professor of sociology at the University of Trondheim (now the Norwegian University of Science and Technology) from 1969 onward. He was also a politically active member of the Conservative Party. He has published several works such as *Educational Systems and the Attainment Process* (1987) and *Educational Reforms and Their Attainment Outcomes* (2001).

9. *Editors' notes:* Christie seems to be mistaken regarding the year of publication of Young's book. The correct year is 1958, and not 1966. Michael Young (1915–2002) was a British sociologist, writer, social activist, and politician for the Labor Party. He famously coined the term "meritocracy," founded the Institute for Community Studies (2005, Young Foundation), and was involved in the establishment of other institutions such as the Open University, National Consumer Council, National Extension College, and Open College of the Arts.

10. For an overview, see Lindbekk 1968.

11. Cf. Lindbekk 1964, especially tables 5a–5b.

12. This seems to be one of the key points for Illich (1969a) and the circle of educators he convened in Cuernavaca, Mexico.

13. *Editors' note:* A more recent examination of these connections can be found in A. Wolf, *Does Education Matter?: Myths about Education and Economic Growth* (London: Penguin Books, 2003).

14. *Editors' note:* The University Library refers here to the current Royal Danish Library, which used to be part of the University of Copenhagen until 1930, when it was subsumed under the Ministry of Education.

15. *Editors' note:* This trend still seems to exist. The global scientific output doubles every nine years, according to R. Van Noorden, "Global Scientific Output Doubles Every Nine Years," *Nature*, May 7, 2014, http://blogs.nature.com/news/2014/05/global-scientific-output-doubles -every-nine-years.html.

16. *Editors' note:* As made clear in his work on restorative justice and social inequality, Christie's skeptical stance toward the open school should not be read in the sense proposed by some conservative educators and politicians—that is, as advocating *one* national curriculum. If anything, Christie's proposed notion of *overview* should be read as a call for educators to promote school activities that are culturally, linguistically, and demographically sustaining, rejecting the naturalization of dominant perspectives in curriculums and schools. Sealing up the bubble, in short, does not necessarily entail creating a similar bubble in all spaces but rather suggests a practice based on acknowledging the values and sovereignty of multiple cultural spaces. For more recent investigations of these practices of recognition and cultural sustenance, see L. Delpit, *Other People's Children: Cultural Conflict in the Classroom* (New York: New Press, 2006); D. Paris and H. S. Alim, eds., *Culturally Sustaining Pedagogy: Teaching and Learning for Justice in a Changing World* (New York: Teachers College Press, 2014).

## CHAPTER 4

1. *Editors' note:* Andenæs (1923–1975) was a famous Norwegian lawyer, publisher, and member of Parliament for the Norwegian Labor Party.

2. I agree unconditionally with Egil Frøyland (1971, 80), who in a spirited article writes that the National Curriculum Committee has set out to create a "school that can be described as a system for the production of preranked and quality-sealed students ready to be funneled into the stations of society where they may best be of service to the gross national product." The committee has—still in the view of Frøyland—prioritized the values of production over the values of the individual, creating a system that places value in their ability to be replaced rather than seeing them as valuable in and of themselves (*egenverdi*). "The committee has chosen to ignore the questionable responsibility of schools to select and rank students according to their capabilities. We will, accordingly, still have an educational system based on selection—or a 'separator-school for everyone,' as Hans Tangerud put it" (Frøyland 1971, 79).

3. *Editors' note:* Christie elaborates on this point—and the general nature and effects of a subject-based school—in chapter 5.

4. *Editors' note:* The so-called Steen Committee acquired its name from the committee's chair, Norwegian politician Reiulf Steen (1933–2014).

Among many other political positions, Steen was notably the vice president of Socialist International from 1978 to 1983.

5. *Editors' note:* Harbo (1927–) was a professor of pedagogy at the University of Trondheim between 1971 and 1982, and the University of Oslo from 1983 to 1997. He is the author of *Introduction to Didactics* [*Innføring i didaktikk*] (1966), and coauthor of *The Struggle for the National Standards* [*Kampen om Mønsterplanen: språk og sak*] (1982) with R. Myhre and P. Solberg.

6. *Editors' note:* Homans (1910–1989) was an American sociologist. He is the originator of social exchange theory and author of *The Human Group* (1951)—where the analysis of Hilltown can be found in chapter 13—and *Social Behavior: Its Elementary Forms* (1961).

7. *Editors' note:* Christie elaborates on and provides an example of this point in the "A Place to Be" section in chapter 5.

8. *Editors' note:* ABC refers to books for beginning readers.

9. *Editors' note:* The references L and R here refer to, respectively, *Lov*, meaning "act," and *Reglement og instrukser for grunnskolen*, meaning "regulations and guidelines for primary and lower secondary schools."

10. *Editors' note:* Jaabæk (1814–1894) was a Norwegian farmer and politician. He founded the Liberal Party of Norway, and throughout the duration of his lengthy career in the Norwegian Parliament, was an advocate for economic liberalism and the devolving of governance to local institutions.

## CHAPTER 5

1. Dokka (1967) describes this as applying to teachers while Edvard Befring (1971) shows that much of the same holds true for university-schooled educators.

2. *Editors' note:* Especially in the late 1960s, an array of new schools with an open classroom design began to appear throughout the Western world offering alternative learning spaces. For a historical overview of changing school architecture over the course of the last century, see T. Hille, *Modern Schools: A Century of Design for Education* (Hoboken, NJ: Wiley, 2011).

3. Within large and dense bureaucracies, specific and isolated solutions often arise, such as the National Council for Innovations in Education, Oslo Youth Office, or new educational centers that are starting to emerge. In these cases, the bureaucrat will obtain significantly more decision-making freedom than is usual within a bureaucracy. This greater freedom leads to rapid growth. But looming within this growth is the beginning of the end: the growth of these specific and

isolated solutions—frequently initiated as breathing spaces within the bureaucracy—produces a separate bureaucracy all its own. The increased size implies that the decisions have consequences, also beyond the scope of the bureaucrats' actual purview, beyond the parameters of the breathing spaces. This increased influence, in turn, will cultivate counterforces elsewhere in the system and undermine their decision-making freedom as soon as the breathing spaces that have been created become visible for others. New breathing spaces will then presumably appear elsewhere. It would be advantageous if such small breathing spaces didn't exist, so the system *in its entirety* would be forced to change in important and permanent ways.

4. Ministry of Education and Research, press release no. 31, August 1971. Here the Ministry of Education would appear to be hinting at reforms that have not yet been incorporated into the Curriculum Guidelines: "As soon as possible, the ministry will aim to abolish the final exam in primary school." This does not necessarily mean that exams and/or standardized tests will be eliminated but rather *may* imply that steps will be taken in that direction. Furthermore, the press release states that "the ministry is of the opinion that proficiency in German should no longer be a requirement for admission to upper secondary school." Something important may happen.

5. For a sharp critique of many of these factors, see Tangerud 1971.

6. *Editors' note:* In recent years, the notion of involving students in gardening, farming processes, and cooking has gained increasing attention. Notably, Alice Waters's collaboration with the King Middle School in Berkeley, California—known as the Edible Schoolyard Project—has drawn attention to the educational and experiential benefits of establishing functional teaching gardens on school sites. See https://edible-schoolyard.org/about.

7. Not only is this self-evident, but it has been amply researched. Roger Barker and Paul Gump are pioneers within this field. Based on extremely detailed assessments of ordinary schoolchildren's behavior within both small and large schools, they document how small schools to a larger degree force students to participate in extracurricular activities. Not only do the students from these small schools participate more frequently in such situations, but they participate more actively and in situations in which they assume greater responsibility (cf. Barker and Gump 1964; Barker 1968).

8. *Editors' note:* cf. the "And the teachers?" subsection in this chapter.

9. *Editors' note:* cf. the "A Place to Learn" section in this chapter.

10. To be sure, the Standing Committee on Education and Church Affairs (Recommendations to the Odelsting XLV, 1968–1969, 8) highlights that "primary and lower secondary school as a whole must be

based on the ethical values of Christianity." With the arrival of the current subjects-based school, however, compliance with this is of course impossible.

## CHAPTER 6

1. *Editors' note:* Here Christie is referring to the Greek word *scholē* (σχολή). For a more contemporary take on the notion of schools as a form of leisure time, see J. Masschelein and M. Simons, *In Defense of the School: A Public Issue* (Leuven: Education, Culture and Society Publishers, 2013).

2. For a description of Vidaråsen, see Engel 1971a.

# REFERENCES

Barker, Roger G. 1968. *Ecological Psychology: Concepts and Methods for Studying the Environment of Human Behavior*. Stanford, CA: Stanford University Press.

Barker, Roger G., and Paul V. Gump. 1964. *Big School, Small School: High School Size and Student Behavior*. Stanford, CA: Stanford University Press.

Barth, Fredrik. 1961. *Nomads of South Persia: The Basseri Tribe of the Khamseh Confederacy*. Oslo: Universitetsforlaget.

Befring, Edvard. 1971. *Studium, yrke og mobilitet. En undersøkelse av norske fagpedagoger og pedagogikk-studenter*. Oslo: Universitetsforlaget.

Boalt, Gunnar, and Torsten Husén. 1964. *Skolans sociologi*. Stockholm: Almqvist and Wiesel.

Carling, Finn. 1966a. *Gitrene: Et Skuespill*. Oslo: Gyldendal Norsk Forlag.

Carling, Finn. 1966b. "Skolen og det likegyldige menneske." In *Er gymnasiaster mennesker?* , edited by Carl Hambro, 54–70. Oslo: Pax.

Christie, Nils. 1968. "Langhåret livsstil." *Nordisk Tidsskrift for Kriminalvidenskab* 56:123–136.

Christie, Nils. 1969. "Samfunnets møte med barn og unge—samfunnsproblem eller ungdomsproblem?" *Norges Barnevern* 46:106–118.

Christie, Nils. 1970. "Samfunnstilpassing eller ungdomstilpassing?" *Nordisk Tidsskrift for Kriminalvidenskab* 58:5–15. Also in *Norsk Pedagogisk Tidsskrift* (1970): 301–312; *Norges Barnevern* (1970): 193–204.

Christie, Nils. 1971. "Scandinavian Criminology Facing the 1970s." *Scandinavian Studies in Criminology* 3:121–149.

Dewey, J. 2000. *The School and Society*. Chicago: University of Chicago Press.

Dokka, Hans-Jørgen. 1967. *Fra allmueskole til folkeskole. Studier i den norske folkeskoles historie i det 19. hundreåret*. Oslo: Universitetsforlaget.

Dokka, Hans-Jørgen. 1971. "En dobbelt utfordring til symposiet." In *Normalplanen, et opplegg til misfostring eller gagns menneske? Foredrag og innlegg fra Norsk pedagogikklags konferanse på Røros 1971*, 61–63. Oslo: Universitetsforlaget.

Eide, Ingrid. 1962. "Noen skolesosiologiske problemer. En organisasjonsanalyse av en folkeskole i Oslo i 1959." Oslo: Institutt for sosiologi og samfunnsgeografi.

Engel, Margit. 1971a. "Et sted å leve for psykisk utviklingshemmede." In *Psykiatrien på skilleveien*, edited by Christian Astrup, Odd Steffen Dalgard, Kjell Nordeik, and Per Sundby, 66–77. Oslo: Cappelen.

Engel, Margit. 1971b. "Human Relationships, Recreation and Social Life in a Village for Mentally Handicapped Adults." Manuscript.

Frøyland, Egil. 1971. "Normalplanen—et politisk dokument." In *Normalplanen, et opplegg til misfostring eller gagns menneske? Foredrag og innlegg fra Norsk pedagogikklags konferanse på Røros 1971*, 73–103. Oslo: Universitetsforlaget.

Harbo, Torstein. 1971. "Grunnskolens nye læreplan." In *Normalplanen, et opplegg til misfostring eller gagns menneske? Foredrag og innlegg fra Norsk pedagogikklags konferanse på Røros 1971*, 41–59. Oslo: Universitetsforlaget.

Hargreaves, David H. 1967. *Social Relations in a Secondary School*. London: Routledge and Kegan Paul.

Hem, Lars. 1971. *Forsøksgymnaset. En studie om forandring*. Oslo: Universitetsforlaget.

Homans, George C. 1951. *The Human Group* [*Menneskegruppen*]. London: Routledge. Danish edition published 1967. Translated by Flemming Balvig Larsen and Jan Zihsen.

Illich, Ivan. 1969a. "Commencement at the University of Puerto Rico." *New York Review*, October 9.

Illich, Ivan. 1969b. "Outwitting the 'Developed' Countries." *New York Review*, November 6.

Lindbekk, Tore. 1964. "Embetseksamenshyppighet blant etterkrigsartianerne." *Tidsskrift for samfunnsforskning* 5:132–146.

Lindbekk, Tore. 1968. "Utdannelse." In *Det norske samfunnet*, edited by Natalie Rogoff Ramsøy. Oslo: Gyldendal.

Lindbekk, Tore. 1971. "Den nye skole i sosiologisk perspektiv." In *Normalplanen, et opplegg til misfostring eller gagns menneske? Foredrag og innlegg fra Norsk pedagogikklags konferanse på Røros 1971*, 15–23. Oslo: Universitetsforlaget.

*Mønsterplan for grunnskolen*. 1971. Provisional edition. Oslo.

Musgrove, Frank. 1965. *Youth and the Social Order*. Foreword by Albert K. Cohen. Bloomington: Indiana University Press. First English edition published in 1964, but without Cohen's interesting foreword.

NAVF's utredningsinstitutt. 1971. "Norske studenter og kandidater ved innenlandske og utenlandske lærersteder." *Utredninger om forskning og høyere utdanning* 3.

Normalplanutvalget of 1967 (Dokka Committee). 1970a. *Innstilling I. Forarbeid til Normalplanen for grunnskolen*. Oslo: Aschehoug.

Normalplanutvalget of 1967 (Dokka Committee). 1970b. *Innstilling II. Forslag til normalplan for grunnskolen*. Oslo: Aschehoug. Published as manuscript.

Reglementsutvalget for grunnskolen. 1970. *Reglement og instrukser for grunnskolen*. Oslo.

Roszak, Theodore. 1969. *The Making of a Counter Culture: Reflections on the Technocratic Society and Its Youthful Opposition*. Berkeley: University of California Press.

Ruby, Bjarne. 1970. "Teknologisk forandring." In *Social forandring*, edited by Erik Manniche, 66–81. Copenhagen: Fremad.

Samvirkekomitéen. 1970. *Foreløpig innstilling*. Oslo.

Skolekomitéen of 1965 (Steen Committee). 1967. *Innstilling I. Om det videregående skoleverket*. Oslo: Kirke- og undervisningsdepartementet.

Sykes, Gresham M. 1958. *The Society of Captives: A Study of a Maximum Security Prison*. Princeton, NJ: Princeton University Press.

Tangerud, Hans. 1971. "Den norske skole i 1970-åra. Hvilke mål har vi satt oss? Hva slags skole ønsker vi?" In *Skolen—et produkt av forskning og teknikk*, 13–28. Oslo: Universitetsforlaget.

Thabault, Roger. 1971. *Education and Change in a Village Community: Mazières-en-Gâtine, 1848–1914*. Translated from the French edition by Peter Tregear. London. French edition, *Mon Village 1848–1914*. L'Ascension d'un Peuple, 1945.

Torgersen, Ulf. 1972. *Profesjonssosiologi*. Oslo: Universitetsforlaget.

Vesaas, Tarjei. 1934. *Det store spelet*. Oslo: Lydbokforlaget.

Wax, Murray L., Rosalie H. Wax, and Robert V. Dumont Jr., with the assistance of Roselyn Holyrock and Gerald OneFeather. 1964. *Formal Education in an American Indian Community*. Stanford, CA: Stanford University Press.

Young, Michael. 1966. *Intelligensen som overklasse. 1870–2033. Om utdannelse og likhet* [*The Rise of the Meritocracy, 1870–2033*]. Afterword by Torild Skard. Oslo: Pax. English edition published 1958.

# INDEX